Technology Standards

Warren W. (Skip) Via, Jr.
Mark Standley

VISIONS™
Technology in Education

Vision Technology Leadership Series #3

ISBN 1-57369-743-5

Visions Leadership Series
Visions Technology in Education
2930 Chad Drive, Suite 200
Eugene, OR 97405
800.877.0858
fax: 541.349.0944
Web: www.toolsforteachers.com

From the Publisher

Visions Technology in Education develops and publishes material for teachers, students, parents, and educational leaders. By producing field-tested resources to assist in the teaching/learning process, Visions aims to utilize technology to better serve students and educators alike.

Visions Leadership Series is an exciting project emphasizing skill training for leaders and administrators who are increasingly introducing technology into the curriculum.

This series provides a map for planning and networking, involving the whole community in the educational process. We aim to link "high tech" with "high touch," as effective leaders recognize the dual importance of educational technology and interpersonal relationships.

We envision a future in which people in the private and public sectors and in education and business, model partnership and cooperation in the educational process.

Dedication

To Zach and Will, the reasons I do everything I do; and to Mary, without whom I could do nothing at all.
    ~ *Warren W. (Skip) Via, Jr.*

To my parents, Troy and Julia Standley.
    ~ *Mark Standley*

Table of Contents

Foreword

Integrating technology well throughout a school system is, at the very least, substantial systemic reform. Research on school reform and restructuring clearly identifies shared vision, unity and focus of purpose, ongoing planning and monitoring, and engaged leadership as conditions essential to successfully implement and sustain significant system-wide change. It is no great stretch of logic, then, that these same conditions are essential for successful, sustained use of technology in schooling.

As a nation, the United States is investing in technology for schools at roughly the same level we invested during the height of our efforts to place the first man on the moon. Often, the human effort expended to effectively implement technology dims even this tremendous fiscal investment. Yet, we are hard-pressed to articulate the benefits we expect to realize by such monumental efforts, and we fail woefully in most attempts to document enhanced learning, performance, and operational efficiency as a result of technology use in schools. We have heard much about the promise technology holds for learners and for educators — indeed for the entire enterprise of educating and learning. It is clear; however, that historically our collective treatment of technology in schools lacks the essential conditions outlined in the first paragraph of this forward ... especially relating to unity and focus.

The world is different, and infusion of technology throughout society is a most profound force contributing to this difference. Not only is the world different, but it is ever-evolving. Think about work, communications, tools, and information, and how these have changed even over the last decade. Then, consider how different these might be again by the end of this first decade of the new millennium. It becomes clear that schools and schooling must be different, too, if we are to prepare today's students for their futures.

So, how do technology standards play into all this, and why is it important for school leaders, policy-makers, parents, employers, other educators, and the community at large to know about technology standards? First, it is important to understand the nature of emerging technology standards for schools and for educators. While most technology standards talk a bit about basic skills and operations, current standards attend much more to improved schooling with technology and to system capacities that foster improvement and innovation.

Foreword

Modern standards are focused on improved school processes, efficiencies, and results—defined by student learning and performance. Strong standards are developed by front-line practitioners and are refined and enhanced by expert and broad stakeholder involvement. Strong modern technology standards document a true national consensus about what the most important technology results and benefits are for schools, how those results can best be achieved, and what supportive conditions must be in place to achieve the standards. An outstanding example of a strong modern set of technology standards is the series developed and published by the International Society for Technology in Education (ISTE) known as National Educational Technology Standards, or simply NETS. ISTE's NETS are included in this book and are available as well at http://www.iste.org.

Technology standards focus on improved learning, leadership, and operations. They define the "what" related to technology that must be woven into the fabric of schooling, and they detail what conditions are necessary to succeed in integrating technology and sustaining its optimum use. So, if we are interested in educational return on investment, it is important that stakeholder knowledge of technology standards and their buy-in to them be as universal as possible.

Technology standards communicate a national consensus that can bring this nation's efforts with technology in schools into focus and alignment, and can, therefore, leverage our ability to address the learning needs of our students for their futures.

In this book, the authors have assembled outstanding resources, identified important issues, and tapped brilliant leaders and thinkers to create for readers a catalyzing piece for considering technology standards as critical tools in ongoing school improvement. In doing so they've made an important contribution to optimizing benefits to schools of technology.

Don Knezek, Director
National Center for Preparing Tomorrow's Teachers to Use Technology
The International Society for Technology in Education
http://www.iste.org
April, 2001

Preface

This book is about technology standards in education. We have drawn from the work done with education standards, instructional technology, and the extensive work being done by the International Society for Technology in Education's (ISTE) National Education Technology Standards (NETS) Project creating technology standards for students, teachers, and administrators. Our goal in presenting this book is to offer ideas, practical suggestions, and connections for integrating technology into the learning and teaching in schools. Even though we refer to various technology standards written at state and national levels, this book is designed to help leaders with the process of integrating those standards into the daily lives of students, teachers, and learning communities.

You will find some important ideas and practical suggestions for integrating technology standards in this book. We have also created a way to allow you to keep current with more ideas and connections on this important topic. You will find more ideas, links to the NETS Project and other technology standards, and updated resources on the Internet at:

http://www.technologystandards.com

The links to Internet resources in this book were current at the time of publication. However, these links can change and some of the printed URLs may not work properly. Visit the book's companion Web site, http://www.technologystandards.com for updates and for additional relevant links. We encourage you to respond to this site with your feedback, technology resources, and links, so that we may continue to build a learning community around this important topic.

Here's what you will find in the rest of this book:

Chapter 1: What are Standards?

It is important to understand the historical, pedagogical, and philosophical context for standards in education to know why there are technology standards. The evolution of standards across many content and performance areas creates the foundation for knowing the relevance and role technology standards plays in education. In this chapter we explore that historical perspective to show that technology standards are part of a larger movement that seeks to improve student achievement through school reform. But technology standards, like school reform, work when they fit within the context of the learning communities, culture, and goals of an organization.

Preface

Chapter 2: Technology Integration — In Search of the Holy Grail

Integration is the Holy Grail of educational technology. Many books, presentations, and resources have been created to help educators understand technology integration. Through many efforts and millions of dollars, the successes and failures for technology integration remind us of the search for the Holy Grail. We believe this is why technology standards are important. This chapter describes technology integration from the standpoint of seeing technology standards in the light of processes around learning, teaching, and school management. We attempt to take the "myth" away from technology integration for students, teacher, and leaders by showing how they each can incorporate technology into educational processes, such as information management, communication, ethical/legal behavior, and instruction.

Chapter 3: Curriculum Frameworks for Technology Standards

Broadly speaking, curriculum frameworks provide the structure and process for translating content and performance standards into instructional practice. Curriculum frameworks might provide instructional methodologies, materials and resources, lesson plans, and evaluation and assessment strategies for teachers, or curriculum planners to take standards from theory to classroom practice. Important terms and concepts such as content, performance standards, benchmarks and computer curriculum are discussed in this chapter to help move technology standards into classroom practice.

Chapter 4: Methods of Teaching to Technology Standards

How to teach with technology raises many questions. Rather than focus simply on the question of "integrating technology into curriculum," we feel educators should ask the question in other ways. It should be "How does our curriculum and our instructional methodology need to evolve to give students experience and success in learning with the kind of expectations that will be placed on them when they leave our schools?" Technology should extend and reshape curricula and instructional methodologies, not simply be shoehorned into existing practice. Project-based learning is probably the single most effective strategy for getting students to use technology as a learning tool. This chapter discusses this powerful method and others that can allow teachers to focus on the curriculum and instruction more than the technology.

Chapter 5: The New R's

Perhaps the greatest challenge in regard to implementation of technology standards in schools lies in providing teachers with the skills to use technology as a tool rather than to teach about it as a subject. It's not just about knowing how to use the technology, nor is it just about knowing how to teach with it. It also involves understanding how technology has transformed communication at every level of our culture, and how students today are increasingly influenced by it. Working with the "Digital Generation" requires new strategies, resources, and relationships for educators. This chapter explores the new skills or "R's" that students, teachers, and communities need to learn to be successful in the new millennium.

Chapter 6: Whose Technology Standards?

Whose technology standards are we talking about? There is more than one technology standard for education leaders to consider—district, state, and national—to name just a few. This chapter reviews the technology standards work done by the International Society for Technology in Education (ISTE) through their National Education Technology Standards (NETS) Project for students, teachers, and administrators. The International Technology Education Association (ITEA) has also created technology standards aimed at technical and industrial applications. This chapter also includes technology links to standards from Wisconsin and Alaska as samples of exemplary standards at a statewide level. It's important to review the depth and range of technology standards that have been written to answer questions of implementing standards in schools, getting ideas for integrating all aspects of the standards in the curriculum, and helping decide whose standards you will ultimately use.

Chapter 7: Frequently Asked Questions

As with most things in life, answers frequently bring up new questions. Technology standards create questions about teacher training, meaningful access to technology, and leadership, to name a few. This chapter brings together questions the authors are frequently asked at their workshops on technology standards by educators, businesses and parents. The implication of technology standards is to create a new school culture based upon ready access to tools for research, problem solving, communication, and collaboration. These questions are reflective of the new challenges and opportunities schools face when embracing technology standards as an integral part of their curriculum and culture. Our answers are a digest of the discussions we have in workshops and are good starting points for conversations with school technology committees, professional in-services, and teacher preparation classes.

Introduction

Technology standards are a part of a standards movement within the education system moving towards outcomes, accountability, and consistency. Technology standards are unique among the standards community in that they reflect both a society's political and pedagogical intentions. Many educators, parents, and community members are uncomfortable with the notion of technology standards. Because of the rapid changes over the past 25 years, it is difficult for us to know exactly what students should know or be able to do with technology. This creates an opportunity to consider the nature of technology as a curriculum subject, the role it can play in the learning process, and the relationship societies have with technology in all aspects of human life.

A definition of technology that floats through keynote speeches and teacher in-services around the country is "...anything that did not exist when you were born." This definition highlights the relational nature between people and the collection of electronic hardware and software we call "technology." The dictionary defines technology as "... the discipline dealing with the art or science of applying scientific knowledge to practical problems" (http://www.dictionary.com). Content or performance standards are usually expressed by "... what a student should know or be able to do within any given subject area."

Whatever definition you use for technology, we encourage educators to remember that children beginning at your school this year will likely not think about technology the same way you do. The computers, TVs, cell phones, fax machines, software, and wireless personal digital assistants (PDAs) are not "technology" to children any more than the chalkboards, phones, or ball-point pens are to the adults. We tend to look at these devices simply as tools for getting things done, for learning, or for play. Which makes it all the more difficult for adults to think about having standards for what learners should know or be able to do with technology.

When considering what students should know or be able to do with technology, we discover five main categories. Students should be able to:
1) operate technology
2) inquire or search using technology
3) analyze data with technology
4) communicate
5) understand/appreciate the role technology plays in society

Introduction

Most of the technology standards written by schools, states, or national organizations place emphasis on these learning outcomes. There are many good examples of standards across the country that we will describe in Chapter 6. What many educators notice about technology standards are the fact they tend to reflect thinking or problem solving skills. Of course standards reflect both, but it's important to recognize that these standards emphasize what students can do with the tools rather than simply knowing the tools themselves.

Well designed and well written technology standards allow students to engage in thinking, learning, and communicating. An educator who understands how to integrate technology into the curriculum will expect the students to demonstrate cognitive activities defined in the standards. The school's curriculum will reflect, by grade level, the appropriate application of the standard or cognitive activity for students. Because technology standards emphasize cognitive activities, they can be integrated into other subjects such as math, art, or science to enhance student learning.

Technology standards are cognitive bridges that allow students to extend their learning across all subjects. Operating tools, processing information, communicating with others, and understanding the role technology plays with a society or culture are important aspects of technology standards for students.

Technology standards exist for teachers and administrators that emphasize use of technology as a teaching tool, a learning tool, and as an organizational tool for professional educators. These standards point to what educators should know or be able to do with technology to manage classroom data (grades, attendance, etc), to communicate with students, parents, and other educators, to integrate technology into instruction to appeal to a wide variety of learning styles among students, and to use technology as a learning tool for professional growth. Technology standards for teachers and administrators describe uses of technology to increase the ability of these educators to be effective at organizing teaching materials, engaging students in curriculum, and communicating with the key stakeholders in the learning community. The implications of technology standards for educators are increased training at pre-service and in-service levels to make them effective at reaching the potential presented by technology as a professional tool.

Whether or not we are discussing students, teachers, or administrators, it's important to focus technology standards around what people know or are able to do with technology. The emphasis is upon what people know and do as a result of technology. The people in education systems learn, teach, research, communicate, collaborate, manage, and behave ethically. Technology can be an invaluable tool for people.

Technology standards create consistent expectations and a common language for information management, cognition, and pedagogy that are important in student learning, professional instruction, school/community relationships, and visionary leadership throughout education organizations.

Chapter 1

What Are Standards?

"What is honored in a country will be cultivated there."
~ Plato

A Short Historical Perspective

The "standards movement" as we know it today began during the Bush administration in the late 1980s. While Goals 2000: Educate America Act (see http://www.ed.gov/legislation/GOALS2000/TheAct) was signed into law March 31, 1994, by President Bill Clinton, the basic concepts were developed during a 1989 "education summit meeting" between then President George Bush and the National Governors' Association. The effect of the law was to set world-class education standards for what every child in every American school should know and be able to do to become successful as an adult in our emerging global economy. The legislation established eight goals:

1. All children will start school ready to learn.
2. The high school graduation rate will be at least 90%.
3. Students will leave grades 4, 8, and 12 with demonstrated competence in English, math, science, foreign languages, civics and government, economics, arts, history, and geography.
4. Teachers will have access to programs for the continued improvement of their skills.
5. U.S. students will be the first in the world in science and mathematics achievement.
6. All adults will be literate.
7. Schools will be free from drugs, alcohol, firearms, and violence.
8. Every school will promote involvement of parents in their children's education.

Educators will immediately recognize Goal 3 as the basis for the current standards implementation in our nation's school systems. Following the passage of Goals 2000, state departments of education began to develop standards for Goal 3. Although technology is not specifically listed as an area in which students should demonstrate competency, most states addressed this area either directly by establishing technology standards for students (as is the case with Alaska, Michigan, and Montana, for example) or indirectly by incorporating technology competencies into other academic and performance areas (for example, Georgia's Technology/Career Education standards, Washington's Technology and Enterprise standards). An excellent state-by-state summary of technology standards compiled by Putnam Valley Central Schools in Putnam Valley, NY may be found at http://putnamvalleyschools.org/Standards.html.

Never Mind Standards — What is Technology?

Before we deal with technology standards, it might be helpful to decide precisely what we mean by "technology."

In the case of the authors' involvement with developing Alaska's Technology Content Standards, we found it necessary to spend a significant portion of our initial statewide meetings defining exactly what we meant by technology. Should we include auto mechanics in our standards? How about Computer-Assisted Drafting (CAD)? An art teacher on the committee even asked about her kiln, reasoning that because it used electrical power, then it must be considered technology as well.

The first filter we applied to that question was one that should be applied to all standards. Each statement of what a student should know and be able to do should be able to be preceded by the phase, "All students will..." Because not all students take auto mechanics, it would not be appropriate to have a standard relating to it. The essential question for developing our technology standards, then, became "what should every student know about or be able to do with technology to be successful in the global economy?"

Upon further inspection, the question of what every student should know and be able to do is not as easy to answer as it first appears. Again, not all students take auto mechanics, but how much should all students know about the technology behind modern automobiles? How has automobile manufacturing affected our economy and our environment? How is society different now than before automobiles became ubiquitous? How, in fact, can you separate technology from any aspect of history, society, or culture? Isn't technology simply what humankind creates to solve problems of survival, self-expression, and advancement?

Given the historical context of educational standards, it's fairly clear that what we mean by "technology" is information technology—computers, networks (including the Internet), and other devices and processes that are transforming our society and our economy by emphasizing the importance of information and intellectual property as capital. At the turn of the 20th century, we were a rural society with more than 80% of our population involved in agriculture. As we near the 21st century, we find that scarcely 2% of our highly urbanized population is involved with agriculture—yet we produce more agricultural commodities now than we ever have. During that time, the Industrial Revolution has come and gone, replaced by the Information Age—at least for now. The BioGenetics Age is already upon us...

It's clear that our society is fundamentally different as a result of information technologies. Not only have the tools of business, agriculture, government, and even art changed, but the basic processes of communication, commerce, and expression have changed as well. Our social institutions are caught in a changing maelstrom of potential, resistance, hope, and fear.

Nowhere is that more obvious than in our public schools.

Still At Risk?

Since *A Nation At Risk: The Imperative for Educational Reform* (see http://www.ed.gov/pubs/NatAtRisk/title.html) was published in 1983, enormous attention has been paid to our public school system, much of it colored by the bleak picture of public education painted in that report. The publication of *Nation* was within the professional life span of many educators teaching today. It's astonishing to realize that since that time we have seen the introduction of the Macintosh computer, the Windows operating system, cell phones, and digital cameras. The Internet—the most basic tool of the Information Age—was a small blip on the radar of a few researchers and scientists in 1983. Protocols that established the World Wide Web wouldn't come along until 1989, and the first graphical Web browser wasn't developed until 1993. One can only speculate what *Nation*'s authors would have to say today.

Responses to *A Nation At Risk* have coalesced at various points into educational reform movements. Some of these reforms came from within education itself. Remember Outcome-Based Education and Whole Language? Other reforms came from outside education or were political in nature—for example, school vouchers and charter schools. Various organizations and foundations, such as New American Schools (see http://www.naschools.org) and the Milken Family Foundation (see http://www.mff.org) have formed to encourage and support educational reform initiatives. The standards movement clearly is an antecedent to the overall push to reform American public schools.

Unfortunately, many educators have become jaded to the "reform-o'-the-day" nature of the process. Pendulums that swing one way tend to swing back (and back again) eventually. Instructional practices that favor whole language methodologies move back toward phonics at some point; bilingual instruction moves toward English immersion, and so on. The result is that instructional practice, in large measure, doesn't change much over the long run. Anyone who went to elementary school in the 1950s wouldn't feel too out of place in most current elementary classrooms.

Are standards just another swing of the educational pendulum?

The answer is "probably not," although we will undoubtedly see many changes in the implementation of standards, benchmark testing, and standards-based assessment over the next few years. Some (e.g., Brandt , R. (1995) "Overview: What will we do with those new standards?" Educational Leadership, 52[6], p. 5) feel that standards are too complex and will collapse under their own weight, and that we may never have national standards as originally envisioned. However, standards have been embraced by virtually all American school districts to some degree. They are endorsed by the U.S. Department of Education. Most educational reform groups support and encourage high academic standards for public schools. Standards, it appears, are here to stay.

What is a Standard?

By most definitions, a standard is a statement of what a student should know and be able to do. This is somewhat misleading, however. Most states that have written student standards have separated their *content* standards—what a student should know—from their *performance* standards—what and how well a student can show that (s)he has attained the content standard. It's difficult to measure a content standard (how would you decide whether or not a student "understands the impact of technology on our society?"), but a performance standard ("creates a Web page with graphics and links") can be evaluated more readily, or at least be translated into classroom practice. Performance standards should flow from content standards, with content standards providing an overall structure and performance standards providing the material for assessment.

But standards are not merely goals and objectives. In

fact, real implementation of standards in a school system should turn instructional practice on its end. Dr. Nick Stayrook, Director of Program Planning and Evaluation in the Fairbanks North Star Borough School District and the principal consultant to Alaska's Department of Education and Early Development for the Alaska High School Graduation Qualifying Exam (which is designed to test student progress toward state performance standards in reading, math, and written language), sees it this way:

> "Traditional instructional practice fixes the time that a student has to learn and allows the learning outcome to vary. You take Algebra II for nine months. At the end of that time, the result might be that you get an A, an F, or something in between. Standards-based instruction, on the other hand, fixes the learning outcome and allows the time to vary. Every student will show mastery of the performance standards, but some of them will show mastery earlier or later than others will."

Read that again. This is a fundamental change in instructional practice that could shake public education to its foundations. In a standards-based system, giving a grade in reading, math, or written language would be almost impossible because what we should be measuring is progress toward mastery of a standard, not performance relative to a fixed time line. Our job as educators in a standards-based system is not to grade students on what they remember over nine months of instruction, but to make sure that they attain the standards set by the school system or the state, no matter how long it takes.

The implications are staggering. In some states, a student can't get a diploma unless (s)he meets the state's performance standards. (In Alaska, these students would get a Certificate of Attendance instead.) Many questions are raised:

1. If graduation is based entirely on meeting standards, can you graduate early? What about Carnegie units?
2. What happens to special needs students, especially those

with specific learning disabilities, that can't meet standards? How might Thomas Edison or Albert Einstein have fared on exit exams?

3. Are exit exams the only way a student can prove that (s)he has met a standard?
4. Will resources for higher-level or special-interest classes (such as drama, oceanography, or advanced foreign languages) be diverted to remedial classes to insure that everyone achieves the standards?
5. Shouldn't students be grouped more by ability than by age in a standards-based system?
6. Should we worry about "tracking" students in a standards-based system?

It's too early in the process to answer most of these questions. Most states are just beginning to adopt standards-based instruction and to evaluate students on progress toward those standards. Undoubtedly, many changes will have to take place before we work all of the kinks out of a standards-based educational system.

What About Technology Standards?

The fact that some states have written technology standards and some have not is evidence that, for most educators, technology standards feel different than standards in other academic areas. Clearly, reading, math, and written language are process-based skills that are used in every curriculum area. Technology is similar to these areas in that regard. The use of technology as a tool across all curriculum areas is the Holy Grail of most technology-aware educators. In this sense, many educators think that we shouldn't have separate technology standards, but that technology skills should be integrated into every other standard area. Others argue that if that's the case, why do we have separate standards for reading, math, and writing? Shouldn't those skills also be integrated into all other standards as well?

Other standard areas such as science and social studies are more content-based than process-based. Standards in these areas more typically require knowledge of the subject rather than facility with a specific process. Many educators insist that we shouldn't be teaching students *about* technology, but rather teaching them how to use technology as a tool for learning. While this is undoubtedly true, our social and cultural involvement with technology and its implications for our daily lives makes it a subject worthy of some study as well.

Even though the authors were involved in developing Alaska's separate technology content standards, we do not feel that there is a clearly right or wrong approach here. Technology needs to be addressed somewhere in a body of standards, either as a separate entity or in conjunction with other standard areas. All aspects of technology—from its utility as a tool for learning to its social, cultural, and environmental considerations—should be covered. It's interesting to note that the technology committee co-chaired by the authors spent part of its initial meeting deciding whether or not we should even be developing separate standards. There was strong opinion on both sides of the issue. We finally reasoned that because most other standards committees had not addressed technology very effectively (they had been told not to worry about it because there would be separate technology standards), we had an obligation to the students of Alaska to do so. That, and the Commissioner of Education told us to.

Will Standards Reform Public Education?

Standards, if they are implemented correctly and if they are backed up with the necessary school infrastructure and teacher development, absolutely have the potential to reform education. If schools can provide adequate access to the right kinds of technology, if classroom instructional strategies move from the "lecture and test" model toward a more constructivism, project-based model, and if teachers are trained (both before and during their careers) in ways to promote constructivism learning, then schools will become vibrant learning communities serving the needs of every student.

Those, however, are very big "ifs."

Public schools resemble Newton's First Law of Motion: "Every object in a state of uniform motion tends to remain in that state of motion unless an external force is applied to it." The more mass and the more velocity that object has, the greater the external force has to be to affect a change in direction. In the 17 years since the publication of *A Nation At Risk*, the various reforms that have been attempted in public schools have done little to jostle them from their path. Schools are enormous bureaucracies that consume large amounts of public money. All that mass is hard to move, especially to move quickly.

Historically, public schools have been the only game in town. If you didn't like them, you had very few alternatives. These days, however; there is a growing variety of alternatives. Cyberschools are everywhere. Homeschooling is growing rapidly—most estimates place growth between 10% and 20% per year. The Internet provides access to more information than would fit into many thousands of school libraries, and it's largely free and kept very current. Many of these alternatives offer students the kind of project-based opportunities, self-paced learning, and scheduling flexibility that public schools, by and large, do not offer.

This puts a lot of pressure on public schools. Many districts are finding that it's some of their best students—those that want to progress more quickly or study subjects in more depth—that are leaving their brick and mortar schools for the alternatives. In a 1998 survey of home-schooling families (see http://epaa.asu.edu/epaa/v7n8), Lawrence Rudner of the University of Maryland found that the median income of homeschool families was $52,000, opposed to $36,000 for all families with children. Additionally, homeschooled children scored "significantly higher" than public and private school students on standardized testing, and their families had more formal education than the general population—not the kind of families that most districts want to lose. This leaves the typically less-engaged students back in the classroom, potentially exacerbating what is usually perceived and dealt with as discipline problems. Ian Jukes (see http://www.tcpd.org/jukes/jukes.html), an educator and presenter with a knack for innovative thinking and foresight, is fond of saying, "When the going gets tough, educators get traditional." We agree. Newton's laws are tough to violate.

It should be emphasized that the authors are among the staunchest supporters of public education you will ever meet. We believe that public schools are the most noble institution in our republic. They have the potential to be the great leveler, the foot in the door available to every citizen regardless of race, class, wealth, or political views. It's difficult to imagine the United States being where it is today without our public school system.

But, circumstances change, and change rapidly. The business world had to come to grips with the new economy virtually overnight. Those businesses that figured it out prospered. Those that didn't figure it out are no longer around, replaced by more focused and flexible enterprises that can adapt and thrive in a changing environment.

The institution of public schools needs to figure it out as well. Standards are a great place to start, but they are just that—a start, not an end. We hope that standards will form the basis of systemic reform for our public schools. They certainly have that potential, and there is little on the horizon that can offer much else—especially considering the competition.

Chapter 2

Technology Integration ~
In Search of the Holy Grail

"TechKNOWLEDGEy — we are as confused as ever, but we believe we are confused on a higher level and about more important things."
~   Alaskan school technology staff t-shirt

Integration is the Holy Grail of educational technology. It is the sizzle behind the hopes, standards, and marketing of technology for schools around the world. Like the Holy Grail, integration is the most elusive aspect of technology for educators in search of increased learning and cognitive gains in their students. If you ever want to see grown adults become shy and withdrawn, simply ask them to stand up in front of their peers and explain what "technology integration" means. The result of this uncertainty is the confusion, inconsistency, and fear associated with integrating technology in schools today. It is also why technology standards are so important.

Do you remember the film, *Indiana Jones and the Last Crusade?* The main characters find themselves in a cave with an old knight guarding a table full of cups and goblets, one of which is the Holy Grail. The scene sets up the problem of the good characters *AND* bad characters having to choose between a range of ornate goblets and simple cups to pick the true Holy Grail. Of course, Indiana Jones picks the correct one after analyzing many choices and dramatically saves his father and wins the day. That scene gets played out more times that we'd like to admit in technology committees and staff development training every day. Educators and school leaders in search of the Holy Grail of technology integration are faced with a wide variety of choices. Some choices are expensive, some are simple, and like the scene from the Indiana Jones movie, the final outcome is never certain.

Technology standards allow us to create a common language and set of expectations about technology. Embedded in the expectations is the process of integrating technology in learning and teaching strategies to all students and teachers. In this chapter, we concentrate on integration and the processes that occur around technology in schools. We hope to break down some of the myths of technology integration and show how it can fit within the processes that make learning and teaching powerful for all the stakeholders within schools. Let us first look at an overview of what "integration" means, and then get specific about what integration means within the processes of learning, teaching, and administration of schools.

The word "integration" has a history in America's school culture. Integration has been associated either with race relations, instructional tools, or curriculum for most of the current teaching generation's lifetime. The desegregation and integration of schools has been an important part of our history and school culture for several decades. The integration of instructional tools involves the ongoing triangle between "technology" (chalkboards, overhead projectors, computers, etc), instruction, and people in schools. The integration of subjects across the curriculum such as reading, math, or science are a part of the pedagogical landscape that shape school culture. Therefore, educators come to the word "integration" with a mixed bag of associations, beliefs, and expectations that are not always easy to know or explain.

For the purposes of this book; however, we want to focus clearly on the integration of instructional technology into processes that occur in school. We encourage you to think about "integration" within the context of these processes to take the mystery and historical baggage out of the word in relationship to schools.

Students, teachers, and school leaders "integrate" technology when they "incorporate" tools into the cognitive and communicative processes associated with learning and instruction. Analogous to searching for the Holy Grail, there are many false and glittery ways to supposedly "integrate" technology. From our perspective, it simply means to bring together the processes associated with learning and instruction with new tools and information to expand knowledge, understanding, communication, responsibility, and creativity. It's not so simple to always understand how these tools and processes will improve learning and instruction. Similar to the debate about whether teaching is an art or a science... technology integration is a little of both.

Integration into the Student's Learning

Students seldom view the technology as "technology." While administrators, teachers, and parents wrestle with "technology standards," students simply go about school learning and playing with friends. Their days consist of interacting with adults, students, and "tools" for learning, such as books, chalkboards, and computers. The path of learning revolves around a series of cognitive processes that shape what they know, understand, create, and communicate. The "Holy Grail" of technology integration for students means using tools that help or expand these cognitive processes.

When they read and use technology standards, most educators are struck with how little they have to do with technology, and how much with manipulating information. As we've discussed in other parts of the book, many educators feel ambivalent about "technology standards." Viewed from the standpoint of "information manipulation" or "cognitive" standards using technology, they begin to make more sense. We encourage you to think about technology standards for students as the wise integration of tools into their learning or cognitive processes. What "...a child needs to know or be able to do with technology" has more to do with information, learning, and meta-cognition than computers. So, let us look at how students "integrate" technology into their learning.

Technology standards emphasize:
* operating tools,
* searching for information,

- analyzing data,
- communicating, and
- appreciating ethical issues.

Technology can be quite helpful to students as they engage in these learning and communication tasks. Still, it's important not to emphasize the tool over the task, the act of navigating over understanding content, or the bells and whistles of multimedia over the message. When technology becomes the "event" rather than the cognitive task, integration is not achieved. Integration for students comes when they engage with ideas, data, information, meaning, and people through the use of tools. The "Holy Grail" of technology integration for students is enhancing their cognitive and learning processes (problem solving, inquiry, collaboration, etc) in a natural way. The challenge and opportunity in engaging students is to center technology integration around these learning, "informating," and cognitive processes that a child does every day.

Integration into Teaching

Teachers carry the responsibility of "integrating" technology in classroom learning and instruction for students. They provide the context for technology within the learning environment of their class and curriculum. They are an important model technology user and ethics coach for their students. They map the cognitive path students travel and find the appropriate ways to fit technology within that path. Finally, they use technology as an administrative tool for record keeping, communication, and professional development. So, why should the "Holy Grail" of technology integration be so difficult for teachers to find in their classrooms?

Technology integration is difficult for teachers for many reasons. Most teachers have received little pre-service or in-service technology training. Class size is often large requiring teachers to stay extra busy simply diagnosing and instructing a wide range of cognitive skills, learning styles, and personalities. Most schools "add" more and more things to a teacher's plate (curriculum, standardized tests, safety issues, etc) without taking away any responsibilities. Technology integration is difficult because teachers have busy schedules and many responsibilities that give them little time to try new ways to teach and help students learn.

The key element of integration for teachers is to use technology as their instructional, administrative, and learning assistant. Technology in instruction can broaden the appeal of presentations to a wider variety of learning styles. It offers teachers new opportunities to expand the walls of classroom learning and makes the process of organizing instructional materials more efficient. Technology in administrative tasks means teachers can use electronic grade books, portfolios, attendance records, and new ways to communicate with students and teachers that save time and effort. For example, teachers can post policy, rubrics, and assignments to their Web pages to improve the communication between school and home. Finally, teachers can use technology as their learning assistant by taking online classes in teaching methodology, learning new software, and/or collaborating with colleagues toward sharing best practices.

Like students and leaders searching for the "Holy Grail" of integration, teachers should remember to fit technology within the dynamic of the cognitive and communicative processes in the classroom. This means that technology is a tool to expand learning opportunity, understanding, or communication strategies. It has to be a natural part of the teacher's style and professional tools. It simply becomes an extension of a teacher's diagnosis, prescription, and communication with students. It adds information, efficiency, learning windows, motivation, and collaboration to a teacher's tool kit. It should not be a baby-sitter, an "add on," or a placebo to true communication around learning. Teachers need time to learn how to integrate technology and make it their own. Doing this means they become better at "informating" classrooms, are more responsive to all learners' needs and styles, and spend more time engaged with all members of the learning community.

Integration into the Leadership

School leaders have tremendous influence over the culture and use of technology in a school. Their personal and professional approach to technology can shape the way technology is used by staff. Leaders are responsible for directing and encouraging staff members, facilitating policy and guidelines, and modeling technology use in their buildings and district. Therefore, it is very important that leaders understand what technology integration means for themselves, their staff, and their students.

Leaders can shape the way technology integration is viewed throughout a building or system through their personal and professional behavior. Leaders' behavior speaks volumes about their own attitudes and philosophy toward technology. Some leaders become the "head geek" and pride themselves in taking a direct, hands-on approach to technology issues. Others act as a coach to the "techies," guiding their direction and budgets, but allowing them to manage the details of integrating technology in data management, instruction, and learning on their own. Some leaders take a totally hands-off approach leaving the question of technology integration unanswered and little acted upon in their building. Because the leader's attitude and actions have such a potentially positive or negative impact, it is very important to understand the ways in which leaders can influence the integration of technology standards across the school.

First, leaders can be positive role models to their staff and students by integrating technology into their job as an educational administrator. Using technology to communicate through email, presentations, and/or Web pages makes the administrator more efficient and effective. Also, as stakeholders see their leader "...walking the talk," it sends a powerful message that technology is an important tool. There are a variety of other ways leaders can shape school culture by using technology for evaluations, analyzing test results, and creating multimedia presentations for students, staff, and/or parents. The essential element of a leader's use of technology is that he/she finds ways to make it work within the context of administrative tasks, which include communication, evaluation, maintaining discipline and safety, motivating, research, and managing budgets. By integrating technology into the cognitive, interpersonal, and business aspects of running a school, the leader sets a positive model for students, staff, and parents to do the same within the context of their role at school.

By being a user, coach, and facilitator of technology in school, a leader can help demystify the "Holy Grail" of technology integration. Their actions and attitudes demonstrate that "integration" means using technology within the context of work and information to increase the efficiency, effectiveness, or the efficacy of a task. Furthermore, leaders can also act as the technology "cheerleader" by encouraging students and staff to use technology to "informate" tasks, create new knowledge and communities, and build new relationships by acting on technology standards that call for such activities. The leader facilitates a culture of risk-taking, not for technology sake, but for building bridges to new understandings, relationships, and learning for all members of the school's stakeholders.

Finally, a leader's actions also sets an important moral tone by modeling ethical and legal use of technology, software, and copyright issues within school. By setting the school's moral tone around technology, the leader emphasizes the technology standards that deal with adherence to law and ethics. The moral compass around technology that students carry with them is as important as the skills they acquire in school. The "Holy Grail" of technology integration for leaders includes a balance between modeling—"...working smarter, not harder"—with technology, the role of coaching students and staff to build new bridges, and setting the moral compass for technology use across the school culture.

Chapter 3

Curriculum Frameworks for Technology Standards

"Technologies do not change schools in any sense worth talking about. Thoughtful, caring, capable people change schools, sometimes with the help of technology, sometimes not, and sometimes even despite it."

> ~   George Brackett
> in *The Digital Classroom*

Broadly speaking, curriculum frameworks (sometimes referred to simply as "frameworks") provide the structure and process for translating content and performance standards into instructional practice. Curriculum frameworks might provide instructional methodologies, materials and resources, lesson plans, and evaluation and assessment strategies for teachers or curriculum planners to take standards from theory to classroom practice.

A quick search for "curriculum framework" on the Internet provides a striking picture of the varying degrees of detail and specificity that different states have furnished for their districts. Some states take a minimalist approach to curriculum frameworks, providing only a very basic suggestion to district curriculum departments about how to devise their own curriculum frameworks, while others provide detailed lesson plans and cross-references to other curricula. Some state departments of education take the approach that it is up to districts to align their curricula with standards, while others take a statewide standard approach.

There probably isn't much advantage of one approach over another. State frameworks would provide some measure of uniformity across districts, but districts could tailor frameworks to their own specific needs or populations.

Ultimately, the question isn't whether or not districts or states develop their own curriculum frameworks, but how the standards are translated through the frameworks into actual instructional practice.

The translation of a content standard into classroom practice is a potentially long journey. Let's start with a broad technology content standard and work our way through to actual classroom implementation of the standard to see how it might work. Obviously, this process and the terminology will vary from state to state and district to district depending on the kind of structures that those institutions have in place. The following is intended as an example, and not necessarily as standard practice.

Content Standard: Students will use a computer to input and retrieve information.

Clearly, this is an intentionally broad content standard designed to be implemented in different ways at various age or grade levels. Keyboarding clearly falls under this standard, as does using a computer's operating system to locate and retrieve information stored there. One might even interpret this standard as covering database use or telecommunications.

In any event, the standard itself is not very measurable. It doesn't specify what method would be used to input or retrieve information, under what circumstances the student is expected to perform, or what criteria will be used to determine whether or not the student meets the standard. Furthermore, it's not specific to a standard benchmark level. If a first grade student were able to type a sentence or two into a word processor, would this constitute meeting the standard?

As we have seen before, a content standard is a general statement of what a student should know. We need to move to the next level before we can begin talking about how this standard actually translates into practice.

Performance Standard: Students will type using both hands and proper home row positioning.

This performance standard is more measurable. It still doesn't give us a benchmark level (are we talking about 3rd graders or 7th graders?) nor does it give us any evaluation criteria, but at least we have an idea of what the content standard is requiring of our students. It's clearly not a standard that we would apply to kindergartners, but we might assume that it could be applied to some degree anywhere from 2nd grade on.

This is only one of what could be several different performance standards relating to the content standard above. Some others could be:

1. Students will use a mouse or trackball to select items from a pull-down menu.
2. Students will save work to their own folder on a file server.
3. Students will locate and use modifier keys (e.g., shift, option, alt, command)

A 2nd grade teacher might look at those performance standards and interpret them quite differently than a 7th grade teacher would. That's the nature of performance standards. They reveal what a student should do, but not necessarily how well or under what circumstances. For that kind of detail, we need to move toward a benchmark.

Benchmark: By the fifth grade, students will type 20 words per minute with no errors.

This benchmark (some states refer to benchmarks as "proficiency standards") clearly states what a student should be able to do relative to the original content standard. We know which students are being evaluated and we know the criteria for success. If a student can type 20 words per minute with no errors by the fifth grade, then (s)he has made documentable progress toward the content and performance standards above.

But, there are still some things we don't know. Under what circumstances should this student perform this task? Will they take a typing test? Will the teacher observe a writing assignment and make a judgment? Will there be only one chance to meet criteria? Will the text being typed be a typing drill with nonsense configurations or a paragraph with real words and meaning? And how do we teach the students to type in the first place?

These are questions that should be answered in the curriculum framework.

Curriculum Framework: *By the fifth grade, students will type 20 words per minute with no errors*

The authors weren't asleep at the wheel. The text of the Curriculum Framework is the same as the text of the benchmark. The curriculum framework does not necessarily add any specificity to the benchmark. It should; however, add elements that help the classroom teacher select materials, provide instruction, and assess the student's progress toward the benchmark.

In the case of the 5th grade keyboardist, we might expect to find the following in a curriculum framework:

Instructional Strategies:

1. Provide 20 structured minutes per day of keyboarding practice
2. Daily fast-writes on a selected topic
3. Use a word processor to keep a daily reading response journal
4. Provide a keyboarding game for free time
5. Allow students to participate in on-line "chats" with other 5th graders on selected topics
6. In a computer lab, conduct one-minute "round robin" writing drills

Tools and Materials
1. Word processing program
2. Keyboarding programs
3. Keyboarding games
4. Computer lab for round-robin drills

Assessment Strategies
1. Keep a daily chart of words per minute and errors; take the top five scores from a three-week period and average them
2. Require at least three scores exceeding 20 words per minute on a timed test
3. Give a three-minute fast write assignment; collect and calculate words per minute for each student

Other Resources
1. Wall posters of keyboards showing proper hands for keyboarding
2. Office personnel who use typing in their daily work
3. Posters or films showing proper keyboarding posture

A curriculum framework should provide a variety of strategies for classroom implementation of standards. The list need not be exhaustive, nor should every element in it be thought of as required. The framework provides suggestions, pointers, and resources for teachers (or for district curriculum committees who are developing curriculum for the classroom) to aid in the translation of standards into practice.

In the case of technology standards, the ideal situation would be to have the standards linked to other curriculum areas that use technology as a tool to accomplish another task. A 5th grade teacher looking at the curriculum framework above might be directed to the social studies curriculum to find activities in that subject that would enhance or extend the technology skill encompassed in the content standard. For example, if the social studies curriculum addressed the exchange of cultural and historical information with students from another state, the teacher might choose to enhance keyboarding instruction and practice by having students enter into a series of real-time chats with another class in another state on some selected cultural topics. It's not difficult to fit a similar activity into a science project (e.g., chat with scientists or exchange data for a cooperative project) or a language arts unit (e.g., have students respond to each others' writing in real time). The curriculum framework provides a vehicle for this kind of integration.

Curriculum frameworks are an essential tool for moving the idea of standards into the classroom. Without this tool, teachers and curriculum specialists will have a difficult time implementing a standards-based curriculum.

But there is one more potential stop in the journey from standard to practice.

Curriculum

A curriculum framework is a collection of strategies and resources. It is not (typically) lesson plans, scope and sequences, or a mandate for specific strategies, methods, or materials. These are elements that show up in a subject's curriculum.

And it's at this point that the unanswerable question arises: Should there be a separate technology curriculum?

Although we cannot find any statistics on this, it's probably safe to say that most educators feel that technology skills should be part of every curriculum rather than a separate curriculum area. There are some compelling arguments for this position:

1. Technology should be viewed as a tool in all curriculum areas, rather than a subject to be studied separately.
2. By teaching technology as a separate subject, we might create a model for "technology teachers" (similar to other specialists such as music or PE teachers), which will draw the emphasis on technology farther away from the

classroom.
3.   Every teacher should know how to use technology, not just those involved in teaching it as a subject.

But there are other equally compelling arguments for having a separate technology curriculum:

1.   Technology skills, like reading, writing, or calculation skills, must be taught and practiced before they can be effectively integrated into other areas.
2.   By having a technology curriculum for every grade level, teachers are compelled to upgrade their skills so that they can implement it effectively.
3.   Unless we have a separate technology curriculum for which teachers are accountable, we can't ensure that all teachers are using technology with their students.

It's difficult to refute any of these arguments, and no one argument stands out as the most compelling. So, what should we do?

First, it's clear that we need to have a technology curriculum framework of some sort. Teachers need to know what technology skills are expected of their students (and therefore what's expected of themselves), and they need to have strategies and resources for using technology in an instructional setting. A well-crafted technology curriculum framework would serve these purposes, even if there is no separate body of technology content standards. Many (but not all) states have developed these, and they can be found with a simple Internet search for "technology curriculum framework."

A formal technology curriculum would take this concept a step further by adding a layer of accountability, in the sense that teachers are responsible for teaching all aspects of curricula for their grade level. It would also set standards for materials and methodology at a district level and ensure that students are exposed to similar methods and expectations across the district if these standards were not part of the technology curriculum framework.

Although the authors are philosophically predisposed against having a separate technology curriculum, we also realize such a curriculum may be necessary during this transitional time in public education. A technology curriculum could aid in gathering together elements of technology standards from other standard areas and presenting them in a more understandable format, or help in relating standards from one area to standards in other areas.

What should go into a computer curriculum? Some computer curricula (for example, see North Carolina's at http://www.dpi.state.nc.us/curriculum/computer.skills/) are more like our definition of a curriculum framework, above. And it may not be necessary to make a distinction between the two as long as the essential elements are clear to teachers, and there are materials and resources available to help teachers implement the standards in a classroom. Perhaps the deciding factor is this: if a district wants to standardize on materials (for example, a keyboarding program or a graphic editor) or on instructional methodology or assessment, then a technology curriculum that included these would be appropriate. If these areas are left up to schools and teachers to implement, then a curriculum framework should be sufficient.

Technology leaders should peruse other states' technology curriculum frameworks (or technology curricula, if they exist) to get an idea about what kind of skills are showing up in those documents. Again, refer to the state-by-state summary of technology standards compiled by Putnam Valley Central Schools in Putnam Valley, NY at http://putnamvalleyschools.org/Standards.html.

Chapter 4

How Can We Teach
to Technology Standards?

"Technology is not a panacea for educational reform, but it can be a significant catalyst for change. To those looking for a powerful tool to support collaborative learning environments, technology holds tremendous potential."
> ~   J.Sandholtz, C.Ringstaff, D. Dwyer
> in *Teaching with Technology*

How many times have you heard this? "We must find ways to integrate technology into our curriculum."

To we as educators, there is no phrase that so completely misrepresents the way that we should be thinking about technology in our schools. The question is backwards. It assumes that our curriculum is just fine the way it is, and it implies that instructional practices do not need to change much. We'll just integrate information technology into our existing structures and go on about the business of teaching the way we always have.

The question sorely needs to be rephrased. It should be, "How does our curriculum—and, just as importantly, our instructional methodology—need to evolve to give students experience with the kind of expectations that will be placed on them when they leave our schools?" Technology should extend and reshape curricula and instructional methodologies, not simply be shoehorned into existing practice.

This will require a significant reevaluation of classroom instructional strategies on the part of most teachers. Teachers will need to adopt a more constructivism, student-centered model of instruction in which students can generate their own questions and create their own knowledge. They will also need to understand something about how information technology has transformed our social and cultural fabric. This is no small feat. Staff development efforts in technology will need to concentrate on these aspects of teacher training, along with specific training in technology and curriculum.

But let's assume (following Chapter 3) that we are educators who have been presented with a technology curriculum framework that outlines some topics that we'll need to cover during the year. How do we go about implementing this?

First, we'll need to think about some projects.

Project-Based Learning

Probably the single most effective strategy for getting students to use technology as a learning tool is to adopt a project-based instructional model. The concept behind project-based learning is to engage students in an ongoing project that involves many complex, interrelated activities. The focus is on the project topic itself—for example, building a structure or doing ecological research on a stream. Students will use math, writing, reading, and technology skills, along with their own prior knowledge to solve problems and create a new knowledge base for themselves. In the process they will be able to relate what they are working on to important concepts in the content areas of social studies and science, and ideally, work in projects relating to fine arts.

Such projects should include the following characteristics:

• Long duration

Some projects may take a few days, but extending projects over several weeks—or even over an entire semester—can provide rich rewards by allowing students to see more connections, and to become more immersed and engaged in their learning. Betsy Smith, a teacher in Fairbanks,

Alaska, spent an entire year with her 2nd–3rd graders planning a trip from Fairbanks to Walt Disney World. The students had to plan their route, buy a car and calculate mileage, find hotels and restaurants, stop at historical and cultural sites, and keep journals of their trip. They used the Internet and other materials for research. She artfully worked all of her social studies, math, science, and language arts activities around this trip. Her Web site http://www.northstar.k12.ak.us/schools/joy/trip96/smith.html includes tips and materials for teachers.

- Cooperative and collaborative group learning, including the teacher as learner

  It's important that students have a chance to interact with each other during projects to share ideas and strategies and to utilize what they already know in the process of solving problems. Students move in and out of the roles of learner and expert as needed. A powerful addition to that equation is having the teacher involved as learner/expert as well. It's rare that teachers don't come away from an extended project with new ideas and insights.

- Self-directed research and inquiry

  Students need time and structure to explore topics of interest. In a group of any size, diverse interests surface and students tend to pursue what interests them most personally. In the process, students learn from each other about all aspects of the project.

- Goal-setting

  Students need to organize themselves and set their own goals. Project-based activities provide an excellent vehicle for this. Journals, planning calendars, and checklists are good tools for this purpose.

- Higher-order thinking skills

Project-based instruction calls on students to do far more than memorize and regurgitate. Students must understand their subject, analyze the problems, develop strategies and solutions, synthesize the results into a final presentation or product, and ultimately reflect back critically on their own work. See *Figure 4.1: Bloom's Taxonomy of the Cognitive Domain*, for some suggestions.

Level	Descriptive Verbs	Possible Technology Applications
Knowledge Student recalls or recognizes information, ideas, and principles in the approximate form in which they were learned	arrange, define, duplicate, label, list, memorize, name, order, recognize, relate, recall, repeat, reproduce, state	• Scan a picture • Use a spell checker • Take a picture with a digital camera • Use good keyboarding skills
Comprehension Student translates, comprehends, or interprets information based on prior learning	classify, describe, discuss, explain, express, identify, indicate, locate, recognize, report, restate, review, select, translate	• Use a word processor to write a report • Select graphics for a report • Use the Web for research
Application Student selects, transfers, and uses data and principles to complete a problem or task with a minimum of direction.	apply, choose, demonstrate, dramatize, employ, illustrate, interpret, operate, practice, schedule, sketch, solve, use, write	• Create a chart to illustrate a point • Create or modify a graphic image • Create an animation that shows a complex process • Select the appropriate hardware/software tools for a task
Analysis Student distinguishes, classifies, and relates the assumptions, hypotheses, evidence, or structure of a statement or question.	analyze, appraise, calculate, categorize, compare, contrast, criticize, differentiate, discriminate, distinguish, examine, experiment, question, test	• Design and sort a database to answer a question • Create a spreadsheet to analyze data • Use e-mail to converse with mentors or experts
Synthesis Student originates, integrates, and combines ideas into a product, plan or proposal that is new to him or her.	arrange, assemble, collect, compose, construct, create, design, develop, formulate, manage, organize, plan, prepare, propose, set up, write	• Create and deliver a multimedia presentation • Present findings on a web page • Create an instructional video
Evaluation Student appraises, assesses, or critiques on a basis of specific standards and criteria	appraise, argue, assess, attach, choose compare, defend estimate, judge, predict, rate, core, select, support, value, evaluate	• Create and defend a performance-based assessment portfolio

Figure 4.1: Bloom's Taxonomy of the Cognitive Domain

Teachers would do well to revisit Bloom's Taxonomy in light of the kinds of technology-related activities that they assign to or expect of their students. Research has shown that students remember more about a topic if they have applied the higher levels of the taxonomy to the learning process, but many of the expectations teachers have about using technology rest at the lower "tool" levels of knowledge and comprehension.

Adapted from http://chiron.valdosta.edu/whuitt/col/cogsys/bloom.html.

- Curricular content, usually across several curricula

  It seems obvious, but the basis for the content of a project should be the curriculum. Ideally, strands from several curricula would be integrated. Conducting a bottle rocket project is a great activity that will engage many students, but if solid curriculum connections are not made, then the project will be a waste of time. We need to ensure that technology-based projects are judged more on their content than on their appearance (see http://www.ed.gov/Technology/TechConf/1999/whitepapers/paper4.html). For example, a student using a PowerPoint presentation as part of a project should be evaluated on ability to communicate ideas clearly, not on the technical aspects of using the software.

- A real-world connection

  Students need to know that what they are doing has a purpose, and they need to see that what they are doing has applications in the world outside of school. Having guest speakers come to the classroom (for help and for evaluation) and going to work sites can help students understand the real-world connection for their project.

- Authentic, performance-based assessment

  Evaluation of student-centered projects can take several forms—portfolios, teacher observation, rating by teachers from other disciplines or departments, project rubrics, and checklists. The latter can be an especially useful tool as a planning/management tool and as an element of the final project evaluation. Some excellent examples of customizable checklists for every grade level can be found at the http://www.4teachers.org Web site at http://www.4teachers.org/projectbased/checklist.shtml. Using a checklist throughout a project can help keep students on task and give them an idea of the expectations for their work.

In the process of being engaged in a project-based instructional approach, students learn to organize themselves, conduct research, solve problems, and synthesize information. They see real-world connections to what they are learning, involve more high-level thinking skills, and develop a context for the skills that they are learning.

Teachers find that their role shifts as well. They become coaches and facilitators, opposed to lecturers and questioners. This role has an added benefit of freeing more teacher time for planning and arranging learning opportunities for students.

In project-based learning, concepts and skills are not taught in isolation. Rather, they are linked together across curricula, perhaps involving multiple teachers or departments, all within a real-world context. It's the perfect vehicle for incorporating standards into the classroom.

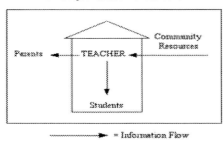

In a typical "stand-alone" classroom, the information flow is usually one-way from the teacher to the student. The teacher is the center of the learning community and is the filter for and dispenser of information within the community.

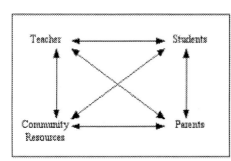

In a project-based instructional setting, information flows freely from one source to another. Teachers are a part of the learning community, not the center of it. Students see increased potential for learning opportunities from a variety of sources, and the classroom is no longer an isolated setting.

Getting Started

Teachers will need to do a little planning for a project. Take into account:

- **Prior Knowledge**: What do the students already know about the topic?

- **Prerequisite Knowledge**: What other knowledge or experience will be required before we get started?

- **Core Concepts**: What are the essential elements that my students should learn about this topic? What are the curriculum connections that I need to make?

- **Instructional Design**: What is the best way to make sure that they all learn what they need? What will be the focus of the project? What kinds of products will the students produce?

- **Evaluation and Assessment**: How can I make sure that they have learned it? Who else can help out in the assessment process?

Teachers who are not used to project-based learning also need to prepare themselves to alter their roles and to give up what some think of as classroom control. A project-based classroom is a busy place with a lot of varied activity going on at the same time. Some students may want to leave the classroom to use the library. Some will need computers to do some Internet research. Some will need the teacher's time for instruction. And sometimes everyone will have to come together and learn about a new topic at the same time, such as how to divide with two digit divisors or how to make hydrogen.

The authors like to think of such a classroom as analogous to a whale-watching ship. Every so often, everyone should rush over to one side or the other to see what exciting discoveries have been made.

The following tables outline some typical behaviors and processes observed in both traditional and project-based instructional settings. Use them as a simple checklist to see where you fall on the teaching and learning spectrum.

Student Behaviors

Traditional Instructional Setting	Project-Based Instructional Setting
Learn the answers	Ask the questions
Finish the assignment	Continue the process
Take the test	Defend your portfolio
Listen to the lecture	Participate in the discussion
Maintain good grades	Meet the standards
Study your subjects	Generalize your knowledge
Read about it	Experience it
Follow the directions	Set your directions
Write a report	Publish original work
Do a science project	Do science
Use provided resources	Choose appropriate resources

Teacher Behaviors

Traditional Instructional Setting	Project-Based Instructional Setting
Stick to the lesson plan	Go with the flow
Require the correct answer	Encourage multiple answers
Expect perfect behavior	Expect developmental behavior
Maintain order	Encourage whale watching
Focus on the academic learner	Teach to all learning styles
Give a whole class assignment	Facilitate individual exploration
Exclude exceptional learners	Accommodate all learners
Focus on discreet subjects	Focus on integrating subjects
Provide instructions	Help students develop their own instructions

Other Strategies for Teaching with Standards

Even in a nonproject-based learning structure, standards can be incorporated into the overall classroom instructional strategy. The same teacher planning outlined above is necessary, and it's important to incorporate as many characteristics of project-based learning (above) as possible. If a teacher is not comfortable embracing project-based learning methods all at once, (s)he could select a single characteristic of PBL—for example, portfolio assessment—and develop some confidence and facility with that before moving on. Consulting with other teachers is also an important part of this teacher's development.

Perhaps the most important area for teachers who are incorporating standards or moving toward a project-based structure to consider is the area of evaluation. Most educators don't like to admit it—in fact, most probably are not consciously aware of it—but the evaluation method we choose goes a long way in determining the kind of instruction that we implement. If we evaluate students by giving them an end-of-unit test asking them to recall certain facts and figures, then what we tend to teach them during the unit is the memorization of facts and figures. To make sure that all of the students get that information, we tend to gather them together in large groups and talk at them, or show them the same films, or have them read the same chapters and answer the questions. In a nutshell, this is a major part of the structure of most current classrooms. We have an assumption of mastery based on attendance. If you attended 4th grade, then you must know how to divide by two-digit divisors because that's when that skill is taught. (The absurdity of this situation is exacerbated by the grade that the student receives. If a student gets a "C" in math in 4th grade, does that mean that (s)he knows how to do multi-digit divisors or not?)

If, however, we chose to evaluate students differently, we might find that we also teach them differently. What if we decided to evaluate students based on a problem-solving exercise that used the skills we taught in a real-world situation?

How would that look?

Let's say that our 4th grade class is studying the ecology of a stream near the school. The students have collected data about animals that they have encountered, daily temperature variations over several weeks, snow depth and ice thickness in the winter, and so on. During this time, they have also been learning about long division in math. As part of the stream ecology evaluation, we might give the students some data and ask them what the average temperature was over a 15-day period, or what percentage of the total number of animals observed were diving beetles. Students would need to know how to use long division to find these answers, and in the context of their hands-on experience with the stream, the answers would be more meaningful and relevant. This could serve as a performance evaluation in math, as well as a way to manipulate data for a science project.

In any case, it's important to let students know to what level they are expected to achieve before they become involved in a project. Make the expectations for success clear. Make sure the students know what you as a teacher will and will not accept. Provide checklists along the way so that students can manage themselves and make an effort to learn what they don't know. Give lots of feedback and guidance during the learning activities, so that students are not surprised at the end of the project period. And above all, learn with them.

Chapter 5

The New R's

"The primary reason technology has failed to live up to its promise is that is has been viewed as an answer to the wrong question."
~ Jane David
in *Technology and Education Reform*

Perhaps the greatest challenge regarding implementing technology standards in schools lies in providing teachers with the skills to use technology as a tool rather than to teach about it as a subject. It's not just about knowing how to use the technology, nor is it just about knowing how to teach with it. It also involves understanding how technology has transformed communication at every level of our culture, and how students today are increasingly influenced by it.

That last statement is very important, and one which many educators fail to grasp. While today's classrooms may closely resemble those of the 1950s, the children sitting in them do not. In *Taming the Beast: Choice and Control in the Electronic Jungle*, (TECHNOS Press, Bloomington, 1999), Jason Ohler emphasizes the need to understand and evaluate the multiple technologies that define our society and our culture—and especially, how they influence our schools:

> "We know them [our literal beliefs] as the 3 R's. But this tag is purely habit, a routine of mind and perception mythologized by a mechanical culture, thoroughly and iconoclastically challenged by the new media.
>
> In the absence of mechanics as the dominant cultural metaphor—replaced for now by the associative meanderings of life on the World Wide Web—the 3 R's are free to evolve. If the notion of 'reading and writing' is deconstructed to its essential elements of 'coding and decoding the symbols of the dominant culture of the day,'

then Webster's definition works well for print, multimedia, virtual haptic environments, and whatever else we might invent."

The problem is that for many of our students the Three R's have already evolved into a new kind of media literacy, while for most of our teachers they have not.

What's The Matter With Kids Today?

As this is being composed in June, 2000, it is still the case that, for the first time in history, students typically know more about a fundamental social phenomenon than do their teachers. The "Digital Generation"—*Wired* magazine calls them the "digerati," some call them the "dot-com" kids—is out there in full force, navigating gleefully among and between global networks, multiple platforms, hand-held devices, new media, wearable computers, and heads-up displays in their glasses (see http://www.microopticalcorp.com if you don't believe us). Donald Tapscott, a Canadian futurist and author, chronicled this generation in *Growing Up Digital*, a must-read for current educators (see http://www.growingupdigital.com).

Members of the Digital Generation (D-Genners), by and large, developed their learning styles and learning preferences in comparatively media-rich environments, using telephones, computers, television, faxes, and other communication devices to explore their world and satisfy their enormous curiosities. Most of this learning occurred in a very lateralized, on-demand basis. D-Genners are used to getting answers as soon as they have the questions, and they don't take well to top-down, one-size-fits-all approaches to learning. If they have to wait too long for a solution, they'll start looking elsewhere. They're used to thinking for themselves—their thinking may be undisciplined or scattered, but it's their own.

It's not surprising, then, that traditional classroom instructional strategies are not as successful with D-Genners as we might have hoped. Ask any gathering of teachers who have been in the profession for more than a dozen or so years if they think that students have a harder time paying attention now than when the teachers began their professional careers. The unanimous response will be en emphatic "yes" if our experience is any guide. Granted, there are many reasons for this, including changes in family structures, prenatal substance abuse, and perhaps an overall decline in general civility. But we can't discount the fact that, simply put, schools are becoming less relevant to this generation. Opportunities for self-paced and self-directed learning are rare. Concepts are presented and usually tested abstractly rather than in a performance-based system. The teacher is the final authority in most cases, and there is usually just one right answer.

The Next Generation of Teachers

Unfortunately, most current pre-service teacher training programs are not doing a very good job of preparing the next generation of teachers. Former US Secretary of Education Richard Riley summed it up this way:

> "New and veteran teachers alike say they do not feel very well prepared to teach effectively to the four fastest changing aspects of the nation's schools—raising standards in the classroom, students with special needs, students from diverse cultural backgrounds, and use of technology. The fact that newer teachers report as much unease as their veteran colleagues indicates that teacher education and professional development programs are not addressing the realities found in today's classroom." Riley, Richard W., NCES Press Conference: "Teacher Quality: A Report on Teacher Preparation and Qualifications." Washington, D.C.; January 28, 1999

That's the government's perspective. What about the private sector?

> "Only a handful of schools of education require their students to be able to design and deliver instruction using interactive technology. Although new teachers are increasingly able to use basic technologies, they are rarely prepared to successfully teach with technology." Focus on Professional Development (1998). In CEO Forum [Online].

Available: http://www.ceoforum.org/reports.cfm?RID=2.
[1998]

We can hope that this situation will change with time, but it's clear that the current task of preparing teachers to understand and teach with technology rests largely with the districts in which those teachers are employed.

The Evidence So Far

Fortunately, there is a growing body of evidence to suggest that making changes in instructional strategies benefits students and teachers alike. Apple Computer's Apple Classrooms of Tomorrow (ACOT) project (see http://www.apple.com/education/k12/leadership/acot/library.html), begun in 1985 and continuing until the late 1990s, asked an astonishingly simple question: "What happens to students and teachers when they have access to technology whenever they need it?" The answer was compelling. Research showed that as-needed access to multimedia technologies (at school and at home) increased student performance by most traditional measures, but also increased skills in areas that speak directly to standards. Students were more engaged in learning, more self-directed, and more likely to use higher-order thinking skills to solve problems. Teachers were more comfortable using technology to learn along with their students, and with their emerging roles as facilitators rather than lecturers.

More recent evidence from a Technology Innovation Challenge Grant program called Challenge 2000: Multimedia Project (http://www.ed.gov/Technology/TechConf/1999/whitepapers/paper3.html) underscores ACOT's findings and shows that students involved in project-based learning activities use more higher-level thinking skills, collaborative learning strategies, and complex problem-solving skills than do students in classrooms using more traditional learning structures. Teachers in project-based classrooms showed significant changes in their roles as well, moving away from traditional roles such as questioning and lecturing and toward coaching and monitoring.

There is also evidence that using technology for

higher-order tasks improves students' achievement in other areas. The Educational Testing Service found that when students use computers to apply higher-level concepts to a variety of tasks, and when teachers are knowledgeable about how to use computers as productivity tools, students show significant gains in mathematics achievement. (Wenglinsky, H. [1998].)

More such evidence can be found in the West Virginia Study (see http://wvde.state.wv.us/news/16). This study of the academic achievement levels of students across the state of West Virginia who were exposed to widespread use of educational technology found that "...the effective use of learning technology has led directly to significant gains in math, reading and language arts skills in West Virginia." This is notable for several reasons, the chief reason being that the students were not using drill and practice or remedial software, but were participating in a statewide program that integrated technology into the overall instructional program. Significantly, the study found that teacher training was a key factor in the success of the program.

This and other evidence taken as a whole reinforces the idea that using technology productively in a standards-based instructional setting produces gains over traditional measures (i.e. standardized testing) as well as fosters a shift in students' skills toward self-direction and organization.

So How Are We Doing?

There is a clear perception that public schools are not properly equipping students for the kind of careers that they will have in the new economy. Some widely publicized studies—TIMSS and SCANS, in particular—support this notion as well. TIMSS ("The Third International Mathematics and Science Study,"conducted in 1994–95 and currently being repeated as TIMSS-R; see http://www.timss.org) investigated achievement in science and mathematics among students at the 4th, 8th, and 12th grades in 40 countries around the world. While U.Ss students performed slightly above average at the 4th grade, their performance decreased significantly at each benchmark level, culminating in an embarrassing overall performance that was "significantly below average" of all of the countries that were studied. (We were actually next-to-last in Advanced Mathematics and last overall in Physics.)

The SCANS report ("What Work Requires of Schools: A SCANS Report for America 2000;" see http://www.academicinnovations.com/report.html), published in June, 1991 by The Secretary's Commission on Achieving Necessary Skills, U.S. Department of Labor, was an attempt to define the skills that our students would need to be successful in the emerging new economy. A solid background in basic literacy and computational skills along with the ability to manage resources, to work amicably and productively with others, to acquire and use information, to master complex systems, and to work with a variety of technologies were all deemed important for students in a high-performance workplace. The primary objective of the SCANS report was to help teachers understand how curriculum and instruction must change to enable students to develop those high-performance skills that they need to succeed. Now, nearly 10 years later, little has changed in most curricula and in most classrooms to assist students in achieving these competencies.

It's clear that we need people who understand and have the vision to use technology in schools to assume leadership roles in the effort to get schools to be more responsive to changing educational and societal needs.

Who Are Our Technology Leaders?

It's an understandable first reaction to look for technology leaders in positions of power or influence within a system. Individuals in such positions typically possess some combination of knowledge, personality, expertise, or charisma that cause others to look to them for answers or guidance, which probably elevated them to that position in the first place.

However, that can be a very top-down view of leadership roles. In the new economy, many enterprises have discovered that relationships among employees are dictated less by institutional rank than by specific expertise.

Management has become more hands-on. Workers have taken on more decision-making responsibilities. Communications have become lateralized and two-way, rather than always coming from the top down.

School systems would do well to follow this example. Leadership is not a function of an individual's job title. A leader is a person who cares deeply about their subject, has broad knowledge of it, and possesses the communication skills to articulate this situation to others. In schools, why would we not look to teachers to fill this role?

What's A Leader to Do?

There are many ways that technology leaders can affect change. The most obvious is by example, and there is no better example to set than producing students who are enthusiastic about what they learn and how they learn it. Teachers who are engaged in a successful standards-based instructional setting should begin by enlisting other teachers in the processes involved in moving toward such an instructional design. Get the support of the building administrator and share your successes at faculty and PTA meetings. Find opportunities to present your ideas at in-services and conferences. Parents are the best ambassadors for a successful classroom. Involve them in your presentations as well, particularly to PTA and other community groups.

And above all, get published. Put your students' projects and data on a Web site and invite others to interact with your students by including feedback forms. For the benefit of other teachers looking at your site, include some tips and resources so that they can replicate parts of your project or begin one of their own.

In the case of technology standards, technology leaders who are teachers should emphasize the connection between their instructional design and the standards on which they are based. Any kind of data that can reinforce your position is important, including student-led assessments and portfolios.

Involving Businesses and Community Groups

The authors have a long history of seeking out and working with business partners in their own districts and we can safely say that, almost without exception, businesses large and small are more than willing to offer services to schools. However, we have noticed a few distinct trends in the relationships between businesses and schools over the last six to eight years that schools should take into consideration when approaching businesses for potential partnerships.

Many schools do not understand the concept of partnerships. In a partnership, both sides benefit in some way. For example, a software company may donate time from some if its engineers to work with high school students in a programming class. The school benefits because the students (and likely their teacher as well) learn new and useful skills. The software company benefits from the potential to have more highly skilled programmers as future employees.

Similarly, a local business may offer to match a fund-raising effort from a partner school to purchase new technology. The school benefits by doubling their fund-raising efforts, and the business gets the goodwill generated by the publicity. Both entities enter into the fund-raising effort together—the business is not simply giving money to the school.

Likewise, a high school multimedia class learning to create Web animations might offer to use their skills to create banner advertisements for local businesses. In return, the businesses might allow their Web manager or graphic artist to work with some of the students on more advanced projects.

These kinds of partnerships benefit everyone. Many businesses, however, are often asked to enter into "partnerships" that are one-sided. As technology has become a more important issue for cash-strapped schools, more and more businesses are complaining that they are being asked to bankroll schools' technology without much in return. We know of a school who wrote several dozen letters to local businesses asking for donations so that the school could buy new computers for their lab. The businesses were not asked to be partners, nor would their contributions reflect back on their participation. The school didn't ask for time, or expertise, or even for used equipment—just for money.

Because of situations like this, many businesses have become wary of entering into partnerships with schools. This hurts all schools, not just the ones who are making such one-sided requests. Many businesses tell us that this kind of request is on the increase.

Districts would do well to formalize the process of school-business partnerships. Rather than having schools, community groups, and businesses seek each other out, districts might hire (or find a volunteer) school-business coordinator. Ground rules for partnerships would be established, and partners could be matched according to need or area of interest. Expectations for partnerships could be set ahead of time, and the business community would know where to go to offer services. Large donors (for example, a company wishing to donate 50 used computers after a company-wide upgrade) could avoid having to make a decision about who gets their donation—the district would have a process in place that would match the donation with a need. If all parties have a common set of expectations and goals, everyone benefits.

How does all this relate to standards? Businesses understand standards. They understand what it takes to do the work of the business they are in. Most businesses are very willing to send their employees to schools as speakers or mentors. They are also typically willing to have students intern or job shadow or simply observe the process of their business. In a standards-based system engaging in project-based learning, this situation provides an ideal way to show students the real-world connection that is so important to project-based learning.

Finding Training Opportunities

The greatest problem facing districts trying to implement a standards-based system is teacher training, particularly when the training involves technology. There are many reasons for this:

- Training is expensive, whether it involves hiring extra staff or outsourcing.

- It takes a long time to accomplish; most traditional teacher training methods—in-services and workshops—are ineffective due to the short duration and detachment from the classroom setting.

- It's never done; the process must be ongoing to keep skills current with emerging technologies and processes.

- Technology advances rapidly, making it increasingly difficult to stay current.

- Teachers job expectations do not include time for training.

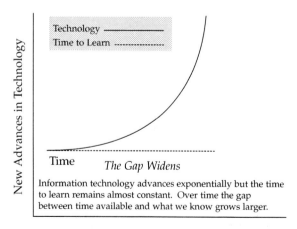

The Gap Widens

Information technology advances exponentially but the time to learn remains almost constant. Over time the gap between time available and what we know grows larger.

Of all of the above, the most significant impediment to effective technology training seems to be the last one. Almost universally, teachers report that the greatest obstacle they encounter in their quest for technology training is time—time to learn new skills, time to practice learned skills, and time to collaborate with others. Teachers certainly do not have this kind of time during a school day, and it's a rare teacher that has evenings or weekends free from additional job-related duties such as grading work, preparing materials, or contacting parents.

In-services are notoriously poor vehicles for technology training. They are too short, typically detached from the classrooms in which teachers are to carry out the training, and too few and far between to make any real difference for most teachers. Summer institutes and conferences are somewhat better—they last longer and tend to be more immersive in nature—but these attract only the most self-motivated of teachers, and districts cannot require attendance at them.

How can we get teachers more training time? There are several possibilities, many of which involve a time-based restructuring of the typical school calendar. (An exhaustive study on these possibilities is available at http://www.ed.gov/pubs/SER/UsesofTime/index.html.)

Send students home early one day a week

This reform has been tried with varying degrees of success in many districts across the country. (Some mostly rural districts have even tried shortening the school week to four days; see http://www.aasa.org/publications/a/1999_03/reeves.htm.) While it can be an effective training tool, it is often difficult to maintain focus and purpose for the time. Some teachers see the non-contact time as a vehicle for completing some of the schoolwork they usually have to take home to finish. Other meetings or in-services tend to fill the time as well. And, parents typically do not like this arrangement, because they must provide for extra child care.

Restructure the school day

Instead of sending students home early, some schools have

experimented with changing the structure of the school day to allow teachers more non-contact time during the day for training. For example, an elementary school might schedule whole-school learning activities one morning per week. On alternate weeks, these activities would be supervised by the primary or the intermediate staff along with parent volunteers and specialists from music, physical education, etc. The rest of the staff spends the time in a structured training program. This shortens the training time to one-half day every two weeks, and the students are in school and doing something useful.

Extend the school year

The National Association for Year-Round Education, a nonprofit group dedicated to scheduling alternatives, has information on a variety of nontraditional scheduling options for schools (see http://www.nayre.org). While the intent of most of these alternatives is to provide more student contact time during the year, many of the schedules can be adapted to provide paid non-contact time for teacher training as well. At the most basic level, extending the school year by adding two weeks to the teacher contract in the summer allows for structured training that could be required of all teachers. A more creative and possibly more effective approach is to have extended non-contact time at various points during the school year. This allows a more ongoing targeted type of training.

Provide in-building specialists

After the problem of lack of time, the most common complaint teachers voice about getting technology training is the lack of in-building expertise that can be called on when questions or problems arise. In-building specialists provide just-in-time training for teachers and help with aligning curriculum to technology standards. There are some serious caveats to this approach, however. It's very easy for this person to fall into a "lab teacher" role and for the computer lab to become this person's "classroom."

Teachers bring their students to the lab, the lab teacher delivers a lesson, and the students head back to the classroom when they're done. The classroom teacher's skills are not significantly enhanced, and the students are taught that technology is a separate subject that doesn't belong in the classroom. Additionally, there is a tendency for this individual to be seen as the "technology expert" with skills and knowledge that are not attainable by "regular" teachers. Finally, it's expensive to staff schools this way.

If this approach is used, it should be made very clear that the technology specialist is a learning/curriculum resource specialist, whose job it is to help teachers plan for and implement technology-based projects in the classroom. It should also be clear that the ultimate goal of this specialist is to work him/herself out of a job by raising the skill and confidence levels of all teachers in the building.

On-line training possibilities

In the last few years, the availability of online training has skyrocketed. The possibilities include everything from free noncredit classes to entire university degree programs. Many on-line classes may be taken at any time during the year and may also have flexible completion dates, making it convenient for just about anyone to find some instruction that is beneficial for them.

The American Distance Education Consortium (see http://www.adec.edu/virtual.html) lists a variety of on-line educational opportunities, including virtual universities. California's Online Catalog see http://www.california.edu) lists more than 2,000 courses from private and public institutions in the state, available to anyone with a modem. Most software companies provide tutorials and other resources online. Here are a few other resources to get you started:

- AOL@School for Teachers
  http://www.school.aol.com/teachers/index.adp

- The Apple Learning Interchange (ALI)
  http://ali.apple.com

- Apple Staff Development On-Line
  http://henson.austin.apple.com/nshelp/welcome.shtml

- Classroom Connect's Connected University
  http://www.classroomconnect.com

- The Global Schoolhouse http://www.gsh.org

- Tapped In http://tappedin.org/

- Teacher Universe Professional Development
  http://teacheruniverse.com/profdev/profdev.html

- http://www4teachers Professional Development
  http://www.4teachers.org/profd/index.shtml

Listservs

One of the best vehicles for staff development is collaboration and information sharing between educators. Listservs, automated electronic mail mailing lists centered around specific topics, are one of the best ways to keep in touch with other educators or professionals with similar interests.

Many thousands of listservs exist on every imaginable topic. There is no topic either too specific or too broad to be represented. Some listservs are one-way informational tools—that is, they send subscribers mail, but do not allow subscribers to send mail to the list—but most are fully interactive, allowing a free exchange of ideas and resources.

It's easy for a district or an organization to set up their own listservs. Free software is available for every computing platform, and it's likely that your current mail server already has this capability built in. If not, or if you want to host a listserv away from your school, eGroups (http://www.egroups.com) will let you set up and administer your own list with no fees.

If you are looking for an existing listserv on a specific topic, try one of these meta-lists:

- CataList, the Official Catalog of Listserv Lists
  http://www.lsoft.com/lists/listref.html

- Price's List of Lists
  http://gwis2.circ.gwu.edu/~gprice/listof.htm

- Liszt, The Mailing List Directory
  http://www.liszt.com

Chat Room and Message Boards

Chat rooms have a somewhat seedy reputation on the Internet. Language in unmoderated chat rooms flows freely and can be quite offensive. Chat room denizens can (and often do) misrepresent their ages and genders, and the unfortunately true stories you hear about pedophiles and others arranging meetings with unsuspecting young people usually start in a chat room.

Some districts have policies that prevent students from using chat rooms, and many districts block access to chat rooms via their firewall.

Having said that, chat rooms can be very valuable ways to exchange information with others in real time (opposed to the email approach of listservs). Most "educational" chats are moderated, so language and other inappropriate happenings are minimal. Additionally, many feature online sessions with well-known educators and authors. If you are new to chats, go to Yahoo http://events.yahoo.com/Net_Events/Chat_Rooms/Education and see what's available. Asking directions in a chat room often reveals other leads as well. Another small but useful pointer to education chat sites may be found at http://www.siec.k12.in.us/~west/edu/chat.htm.

Message boards are similar to chat rooms and listservs in many regards, but they are not real-time exchanges. In fact, they are simply virtual bulletin boards on which participants can post notes or questions and receive responses. Check the 21st Century Teachers Network's Teacher-to-Teacher message boards at http://21ct.org and Learning.Com's Discussion Boards for good examples. Also visit Teachers.Net's array of chat rooms, message boards, and other resources for educators at http://teachers.net.

Grants for Professional Development

It's not easy to write grants. They take time, require research, and typically involve partnerships and cooperative efforts that can be difficult to coordinate. And nothing is more discouraging than spending all of that time and effort without receiving funding in a competitive grant.

However, there is grant money available for a variety of purposes, much of it relating to standards, technology, and staff development. The U.S. Department of Education's Web site includes a section called Funding Opportunities (see http://www.ed.gov/funding.html) that provides a great deal of information about how to write grants and places to look for funding. It's an important place to start if you are new to grant writing, or if you are looking for new possibilities for funding sources. USDOE's Technology Innovation Challenge Grants (see http://www.ed.gov/Technology/challenge) annually provides millions of dollars for districts and partners to create and implement innovative teacher training programs.

The Federal Money Retriever (see http://www.fedmoney.com) provides a clearinghouse of federal money in various categories. A recent glance at the teacher education and training section revealed 36 different grants for a variety of federal priorities. The Bill and Melinda Gates Foundation (see http://www.gatesfoundation.org/learning/education)

offers grants targeted at school leadership, high school achievement, and minority education, though these categories may change from time to time. Another very comprehensive resource for grants and funding may be found at http://www.unc.edu/cit/guides/irg-07.html. This site contains tips, print resources, and links to a large variety of organizations.

Below are some additional sites that provide links to funding sources for educators:

- Kathy Schrock's Grant Sources for Educators
  http://school.discovery.com/schrockguide/business/grants.html

- Grants and Related Resources from Michigan State University
  http://www.lib.msu.edu/harris23/grants/grants.htm

- Resource Pages for Educational Grant Seekers from the Columbia Education Center
  http://www.col-ed.org/fund

Many states offer targeted grants to districts for teacher training. Check your state's Department of Education Web site for information.

Generally speaking, most grants won't pay for equipment unless that equipment is used in an innovative program for teacher training or student achievement. This is as it should be. We should be focusing on the use of technology and not in the technology itself.

Obviously, there are many resources for educators, school boards, and communities to consider when thinking about training teachers to teach with technology. Creative combinations of these resources can result in effective training and, ultimately, increased student performance. It's imperative that districts consider teacher training as the cornerstone of any effort at technology-based school reform efforts.

Chapter 6

Whose Technology Standards?

"Technology standards? Why do we need technology standards? We don't have pencil standards, do we?"
                            ~   Educator at authors' workshop

One of the key issues in understanding and using technology standards in the classroom will be the answer to the question, "Whose technology standards should we use?" Most schools should be accountable for implementing their district or state standards, but as you will soon discover not all technology standards are created equal. In addition, there are technology standards developed by national organizations, such as The International Society for Technology in Education (ISTE) and The International Technology Education Association. There are important differences in the technology standards among states and the national groups.

For purposes of this book, we chose to focus on two of the national organizations and two of the states' technology standards. With permission of the organizations and states, we have linked these standards from their respective Web sites and provided the URLs. It's helpful to compare these standards, their varied approaches to what a student should "know or be able to do with technology," and the implications for teaching and staff development. For a complete analysis of the national organizations' standards, we encourage you to purchase a copy of their Standards books, which provide in-depth lesson plans, resource guides, and discussion about integrating technology into the curriculum.

International Society for Technology in Education (ISTE) (www.iste.org)

The International Society for Technology in Education (ISTE) is a "… nonprofit professional organization with a worldwide membership of technology-using educators." This international group focuses on resources, research, publishing, and workshops for the improvement of education through the integration of computer-based technology in the curriculum. They are working on leadership projects funded through grants and industry partnerships that span the spectrum of curriculum ideas, research, and staff development in educational technology. Through sponsorships from the U.S. Department of Education, NASA, the Milken Exchange on Education, and Apple Computer, Inc, ISTE and partners have developed for the National Educational Technology Standards (NETS) project working to establish technology standards for students, teachers, and administrators.

National Educational Technology Standards (NETS) (http://cnets.iste.org/index.html)

The NETS-S are national educational technology standards for students and the NETS-T are national educational technology standards for teachers.

National Educational Technology Standards for Students (NETS-S)

The NETS-S document titled *National Educational Technology Standards for Students — Connecting Curriculum and Technology,* published by ISTE (ISBN 1-56484-150-20), is a 373-page book containing foundation standards for students, profiles for technology literate students, performance indicators, curriculum examples, and teaching scenarios for technology and learning. This book is an important and rich resource for educators and students nationwide.

With permission from ISTE, we present a description and complete list of the foundation standards for students and teachers. Notice the emphasis on collaboration, problem solving, communication, and learning skills in these standards that answer the question, "…what students should know or be able to do with technology?"

"The technology foundation standards for students are divided into six broad categories. Standards within each category are to be introduced, reinforced, and mastered by students. These categories provide a framework for linking performance indicators within the Profiles for Technology Literate Students to the standards. Teachers can use these standards and profiles as guidelines for planning technology-based activities in which students achieve success in learning, communication, and life skills." (from pages 14–15).

For a more in-depth description of performance indicators, Profiles for Technology Literate Students, and standards, ISTE's National Educational Technology Standards for Students — Connecting Curriculum and Technology *is an excellent and highly recommended resource. You can find this book and other important technology standards references listed on page 87 at the back of this book.*

Student Standards

1. Basic operations and concepts
    *   Students demonstrate a sound understanding of the nature and operation of technology systems.
    *   Students are proficient in the use of technology.

2. Social, ethical, and human issues
    *   Students understand the ethical, cultural, and societal issues related to technology.
    *   Students practice responsible use of technology systems, information, and software.
    *   Students develop positive attitudes toward technology uses that support lifelong learning, collaboration, personal pursuits, and productivity.

3. Technology productivity tools
    *   Students use technology tools to enhance learning, increase productivity, and promote creativity.

- Students use productivity tools to collaborate in constructing technology-enhanced models, prepare publications, and produce other creative works.

4. Technology communications tools
   - Students use telecommunications to collaborate, publish, and interact with peers, experts, and other audiences.
   - Students use a variety of media and formats to communicate information and ideas effectively to multiple audiences.

5. Technology research tools
   - Students use technology to locate, evaluate, and collect information from a variety of sources.
   - Students use technology tools to process data and report results.
   - Students evaluate and select new information resources and technological innovations based on the appropriateness for specific tasks.

6. Technology problem-solving and decision-making tools
   - Students use technology resources for solving problems and making informed decisions.
   - Students employ technology in the development of strategies for solving problems in the real world.

National Educational Technology Standards for Teachers (NETS-T)

ISTE also developed technology standards for teachers through the NETS project. These standards are listed below and reflect ISTE's stated purpose... "Being prepared to use technology and knowing how that technology can support student learning must become integral skills in every teacher's professional repertoire." Their emphasis focuses on teachers acquiring new skills, creating new learning environments, and being able to use the ISTE performance indicators to measure their growth.

The NETS-T book from ISTE includes important resources to help teachers and teacher preparation programs (pre-service and in-service) "...establish new learning environments, help students apply strategies for solving problems, and to use appropriate tools for learning." The NETS-T book includes essential conditions for teacher preparation, technology standards and performance indicators for teachers, technology performance profiles for teacher preparation and technology literate teachers, and scenarios for student teaching/internships performance profiles. This rich resource is a "must have" for teachers, districts, staff development, and teacher preparation programs to fully benefit from all the work, reflection, thought, and practical ideas in the ISTE Standards for Teachers book.

Teacher Standards

I. TECHNOLOGY OPERATIONS AND CONCEPTS
Teachers demonstrate a sound understanding of technology operations and concepts.

Teachers:
A. demonstrate introductory knowledge, skills, and understanding of concepts related to technology (as described in the ISTE National Education Technology Standards for Students).
B. demonstrate continual growth in technology knowledge and skills to stay abreast of current and emerging technologies.

II. PLANNING AND DESIGNING LEARNING ENVIRONMENTS AND EXPERIENCES
Teachers plan and design effective learning environments and experiences supported by technology.

Teachers:
A. design developmentally appropriate learning opportunities that apply technology-enhanced instructional strategies to support the diverse needs of learners.
B. apply current research on teaching and learning with

Technology Standards   61 technology when planning learning environments and experiences.

C. identify and locate technology resources and evaluate them for accuracy and suitability.
D. plan for the management of technology resources within the context of learning activities.
E. plan strategies to manage student learning in a technology-enhanced environment.

III. TEACHING, LEARNING, AND THE CURRICULUM

Teachers implement curriculum plans that include methods and strategies for applying technology to maximize student learning.

Teachers:

A. facilitate technology-enhanced experiences that address content standards and student technology standards.
B. use technology to support learner-centered strategies that address the diverse needs of students.
C. apply technology to develop students' higher order skills and creativity
D. manage student learning activities in a technology-enhanced environment.

IV. ASSESSMENT AND EVALUATION

Teachers apply technology to facilitate a variety of effective assessment and evaluation strategies.

Teachers:

A. apply technology in assessing student learning of subject matter using a variety of assessment techniques.
B. use technology resources to collect and analyze data, interpret results, and communicate findings to improve instructional practice and maximize student learning.
C. apply multiple methods of evaluation to determine students' appropriate use of technology resources for learning, communication, and productivity.

V. PRODUCTIVITY AND PROFESSIONAL PRACTICE

Teachers use technology to enhance their productivity and professional practice.

Teachers:
A. use technology resources to engage in ongoing professional development and lifelong learning.

B. continually evaluate and reflect on professional practice to make informed decisions regarding the use of technology in support of student learning.

C. apply technology to increase productivity.

D. use technology to communicate and collaborate with peers, parents, and the larger community to nurture student learning.

VI. SOCIAL, ETHICAL, LEGAL, AND HUMAN ISSUES
Teachers understand the social, ethical, legal, and human issues surrounding the use of technology in PK–12 schools and apply those principles in practice.

Teachers:
A. model and teach legal and ethical practice related to technology use.
B. apply technology resources to enable and empower learners with diverse backgrounds, characteristics, and abilities.
C. identify and use technology resources that affirm diversity.
D. promote safe and healthy use of technology resources.
E. facilitate equitable access to technology resources for all students.

Technology Standards for School Administrators (TSSA)

The collaborative for Technology Standards for School Administrators (TSSA Collaborative) is leading an initiative to develop and document a national consensus about what PK–12 administrators should know about and be able to do to optimize benefits of technology use in schools. This consensus will be published by the Collaborative in October 2001; however, the draft standards may be viewed and commented on at the ISTE Web site at www.iste.org.

The effort is grounded in the belief that effective implementation of technology in all facets of an educational system is, in itself, large-scale systemic reform. There is clear and critical evidence of the key role leadership plays in successful school reform. Therefore, the Collaborative's standards will identify a common focus for the role of leadership in enhancing learning and school operations through the use of technology. More fundamentally, the Collaborative addresses leadership for technology with the ultimate purpose of preparing students for their futures.

These standards present targets for school administrators. They are indicators of effective leadership for technology in schools. They define neither the minimum nor maximum level of knowledge and skills required of a leader, and are neither a comprehensive laundry list nor a guaranteed recipe for effective technology leadership. Rather, these standards represent a national consensus among educational stakeholders of what best indicates effective school leadership for comprehensive and effective use of technology in schools. The standards should stretch almost every school administrator in some areas, yet each individual standard is attainable by the accomplished educational leader. Although a national consensus, in no way are these meant to inhibit new development, innovation, or progress for schools or for school leadership.

The TSSA Collaborative and the myriad of professionals who have contributed to this effort to date openly acknowledge the wide range of roles administrators play in schools, even when titles are similar. School and system size, degree of site-based governance, community characteristics, and strengths of individual administrators are but a few of the parameters that may cause variations in actual job roles. For this reason, these standards must be used in a way that acknowledges the local context of school leadership. Wise consumers of these standards and indicators must acknowledge a responsibility to apply this national resource appropriately within the local context.

A rich array of expectations exists for use of these standards. Drawing from individuals, institutions, firms, and other organizations that have expressed keen interest in the TSSA Standards, these standards will find application in:

- pre-service and in-service program design
- assessment and evaluation
- role definition and job descriptions
- individual and system accountability
- accreditation of schools and of administrator preparation programs
- certification (credentialing) of administrators
- self-assessment and goal setting
- design of technology tools for school administrators

The audiences to which these standards must communicate are equally varied. Obviously, school boards, administrators, human resources staff, staff developers, higher education faculty, and state department educators will make use of this resource. Some audiences that may not be so obvious; however, include state and federal policy-makers, industry representatives and service providers, professional organizations, parents, taxpayers, and other community constituents. This places priority, then, on clarity and simplicity of language, free from specific education jargon. For example, the performance indicator, "allocate financial and human resources to ensure full implementation of the technology plan" encourages leadership to understand concepts such as total cost of ownership and total cost of management if those are the current sets of principles that are receiving emphasis. The wording choice communicates to a variety of audiences, and it also encourages accomplished leaders to stay current as strategies and accepted principles evolve.

There is consensus as well among those participating in the early stages of TSSA development that an underlying assumption to these standards should be explicitly stated. Administrators should be competent users of information and technology tools that are common to information-age professionals. That is, they must be "doers" with technology. It is not "okay" or "understandable" for school administrators to have a support person "do" the email for them or "manipulate" the assessment data and "bring" them the summary. Certainly, technology empowers administrators by the information it can practically produce and communicate, but it empowers the administrator many-fold who masters the tools and processes that allow him/her to be creative with its use first hand and to work with information dynamically.

The vision of the TSSA Collaborative is that the Technology Standards for School Administrators will identify knowledge and skills that constitute the "core"—what every PK–12 administrator needs regardless of specific job role—and, then extend that core to the specific needs of administrators in each of three job roles: (1) superintendent and cabinet-level leaders, (2) district-level leaders for content-specific or other district programs, and (3) campus-level leaders including principals and assistant principals. This phase of the effort does not address role-specific standards for business officers or technology directors.

The Technology Standards for School Administrators (TSSA) Collaborative represents significant project stakeholders who are committed to producing a set of standards necessary for school administrators to ensure effective use of technology in schools. Collaborative members include the National School Boards Association (NSBA), National Association of Elementary School Principals (NAESP), the National Association of Secondary School Principals (NASSP), the International Society for Technology in Education (ISTE), the Consortium for School Networking (CoSN), the North Central Regional Technology Consortium/North Central Regional Educational Laboratory, the Southern Regional Education Board (SREB), the Kentucky Department of Education, the Mississippi Department of Education, the Principals' Executive Program–University of North Carolina, and the College of Education–Western Michigan University.

The TSSA Standards Project is funded by the U.S. Department of Education's "Preparing Tomorrow's Teachers to Use Technology" (PT3) Program and from the TSSA project contributors. Project management is provided by the International Society for Technology in Education (ISTE).

For additional information about the TSSA project contact:

Don Knezek, Director
TSSA Standards Project
ISTE's NCPT3
University of North Texas
dknezek@iste.org

Heidi Rogers, Co-Director
TSSA Standards Project
ISTE President
University of Idaho Coeur d'Alene
hrogers@uidaho.edu

James Bosco, Chair
TSSA Collaborative
College of Education
Western Michigan University
 bosco@wmich.edu

International Technology Education Association (ITEA)
www.iteawww.org

The International Technology Education Association based in Reston, Virginia represents another national perspective on technology education. This group, through a project titled "Technology for All Americans," created technology literacy standards in a 248-page document called "Standards for Technological Literacy." This project and standards were supported by the ITEA, NASA, National Science Foundation, and other partnerships with schools and businesses. With ITEA's permission we have reproduced the 20 technology standards which answer "...what every student should know or be able to do with technology." Please notice the emphasis in these standards on technology literacy. The book also contains vignettes, compendiums, resources, and rich descriptions of the standards.

"Technology Content Standards is designed as a guide for educating students in developing technological literacy. Technological literacy is the ability to use, manage, assess, and understand technology." (page 9)

TECHNOLOGY CONTENT STANDARDS

The Nature of Technology

Standard 1: Students will develop an understanding of the characteristics and scope of technology.

Standard 2: Students will develop an understanding of the core concepts of technology.

Standard 3: Students will develop an understanding of the relationships among technologies and the connections between technology and other fields of study.

Technology and Society

Standard 4: Students will develop an understanding of the cultural, social, economic, and political effects of technology.

Standard 5: Students will develop an understanding of the effects of technology on the environment.

Standard 6: Students will develop an understanding of the role of society in the development and use of technology.

Standard 7: Students will develop an understanding of the influence of technology on history.

Design

Standard 8:   Students will develop an understanding of the attributes of design.

Standard 9:   Students will develop an understanding of engineering design.

Standard 10:   Students will develop an understanding of the role of troubleshooting, research and development, invention and innovation, and experimentation in problem solving.

Abilities of a Technological World

Standard 11:   Students will develop abilities to apply the design process.

Standard 12:   Students will develop abilities to use and maintain technological products and systems.

Standard 13:   Students will develop abilities to assess the impact of products and systems.

The Designed World

Standard 14:   Students will develop an understanding of and be able to select and use medical technologies.

Standard 15:   Students will develop an understanding of and be able to select and use agricultural and related biotechnologies.

Standard 16:   Students will develop an understanding of and be able to select and use energy and power technologies.

Standard 17:   Students will develop an understanding of and be able to select and use information and communication technologies.

Standard 18:   Students will develop an understanding of and be able to select and use transportation technologies.

Standard 19:   Students will develop an understanding of and be able to select and use manufacturing technologies.

Standard 20:   Students will develop an understanding of and be able to select and use construction technologies.

STATE STANDARDS

Alaska Technology Content Standards
www.educ.state.ak.us/ContentStandards/home.html

Standard 1
A student should be able to operate technology-based tools.

A student who meets the content standard should:
1. use a computer to enter and retrieve information;
2. use technological tools for learning, communications, and productivity;
3. use local and worldwide networks;
4. manage and maintain technology tools; and
5. diagnose and solve common technology problems.

Standard 2
A student should be able to use technology to locate, select, and manage information.

A student who meets the content standard should:
1. identify and locate information sources using technology;
2. choose sources of information from a variety of media; and
3. select relevant information by applying accepted research methods.

Standard 3
A student should be able to use technology to explore ideas, solve problems, and derive meaning.

A student who meets the content standard should:
1. use technology to observe, analyze, interpret, and draw conclusions;
2. solve problems both individually and with others; and
3. create new knowledge by evaluating, combining, or extending information using multiple technologies.

Standard 4

A student should be able to use technology to express ideas and exchange information.

A student who meets the content standard should:
1. convey ideas to a variety of audiences using publishing, multimedia, and communications tools;
2. use communications technology to exchange ideas and information; and
3. use technology to explore new and innovative methods for interaction with others.

Standard 5

A student should be able to use technology responsibly and understand its impact on individuals and society.

A student who meets the content standard should:
1. evaluate the potentials and limitations of existing technologies;
2. discriminate between responsible and irresponsible uses of technology;
3. respect others' rights of privacy in electronic environments;
4. demonstrate ethical and legal behavior regarding intellectual property, which is the manifestation of an original idea, such as computer software, music, or literature;
5. examine the role of technology in the workplace and explore careers that require the use of technology;
6. evaluate ways that technology impacts culture and the environment;
7. integrate the use of technology into daily living; and
8. recognize the implications of emerging technologies.

Wisconsin's Model Academic Standards for Technology in Education

www.dpi.state.wi.us/standards/index.html

Although not listed here, the State of Wisconsin has developed Model Academic Standards for a variety of curriculum areas, including technology. These standards are good examples and answers for Wisconsin students about what they should know or be able to do with technology. To view the Wisconsin standards online, visit their Web site listed on the previous page. Please note the rationales for each content standard.

The rationales are important in the process of creating the vision and justification for the standards, although the rationales typically do not show up in the legislation, state policy, or the brochures/pamphlets for public consumption. In our minds the rationales are very important to understand the mind-set of the group putting the state standards together.

We applaud Wisconsin for including theirs in the Academic Standards documents, as well as the job they did putting together useful content and performance standards for technology education.

When thinking about creating and using technology standards in education, it is important to consider "whose technology standards" you will be considering.

As we mentioned earlier, most educators will be predisposed to use their state content standards, which may or may not have a separate technology standard. Some states, like Alaska, will have content standards, but not performance standards. Others will have content and performance standards, but not the frameworks aimed specifically at technology. So, what do we recommend you do about working in this area of technology standards?

The area of technology standards is a broad arena containing national, state, and local answers to the questions "...what students should know and be able to do with technology." We strongly encourage you to acquire, and then study the documents on Technology Standards from ISTE and ITEA. An incredible wealth of ideas and thinking have gone into these standards for students. Next, you will want to consider sampling other state standards for ideas about technology literacy and information literacy that don't show up in the national standards. Finally, you will want to glean from all of these sources the most relevant and appropriate standards for your school system and students.

Most standards center around information or technology literacy, but there are many opportunities within the technology standards to teach collaboration, research, communication, problem solving, and higher order thinking skills. Another aspect to technology standards is the opportunity to integrate them into core curriculum areas such as math, reading, writing, science, social studies, art, languages, or music. We are in favor of integrating technology as much as possible across the curriculum so that technology education does not become an "event" in the students' day, but rather a bridge-building tool throughout their explorations in learning.

As with most things in education, it is very important that schools identify "...what students should know and be able to do with technology." These answers become the technology standards that should be integrated across the curriculum. They should become the language and culture of the learning community and the driving force behind staff development, as well as one of the school administrator's top goals.

With these conditions in a school setting it is possible for all learners (students and faculty) to focus not only on the tools, but on what the technology can do to give wings to the ideas, stories, and voices of every child.

Chapter 7

Frequently Asked Questions

"Powerful questioning is the answer."
~ Jamie MacKenzie

How do we improve access to technology for our students?

Technology access is a very important issue in regard to achieving technology standards. It goes without saying that students need meaningful access to technology to learn through it. A lot of worthwhile attention has been paid to the digital divide within our country. Many other countries around the world have the same problems as students and families with access and those without. What can we do?

Funding and prioritization of access to technology are two of the largest hurdles schools must overcome to make gains for students. The federal government has been putting a lot of funding into technology through grants, e-rate projects, and federal entitlement programs. Make sure your school is taking advantage of the myriad of federal grants available in this area. Check out the U.S. Department's Web site (www.ed.gov) for resources and grant opportunities.

Other areas of state and local funding for technology come through bonds, technology levies, special allocations, capital appropriations, and other sources. Research all available state and local budgets for opportunities to fund technology through these funds to create more access. Many schools also use PTAs and school/business partnerships to increase access to technology for students through fund-raising or partnership projects.

But let's think about "meaningful access" to technology. Practically speaking, that could mean *access* to technology for students 7 days a week/24 hours a day. We emphasize *access* because we don't advocate "use" on this time scale. Wealthier families can provide 24/7 access to technology for their children, but how do we accomplish this for ALL students in our learning communities? Some of the obvious strategies include more technology in schools (classroom/labs), in local libraries, and after-school programs in the community. What are other ways can we make technology more accessible to students?

First, establish "meaningful technology access" as a school-wide and community-wide goal. This means having a meaningful technology plan, or as we like to say, an "information literacy plan," which describes in detail how students learn to become information literate in school. This includes using technology as an information literacy tool that helps all students within the learning community. Sell the benefits of "information literacy" to the community through innovative and service-oriented projects that benefit the larger community. Once the community is aware of the benefits and power of technology in information-literate students, they will be more willing to "buy in" to creating meaningful access. Marketing the learning students achieve through technology create more acceptance for creating more access.

Next, create targets for access to technology for learners at school. We feel it's important that every teacher/administrator first have meaningful access to technology with appropriate staff development. Create a goal in which every staff member has technology and set expectations about what they will achieve as a result (email to parents, a homework Web page, electronic grade books, etc.). Then, back it up with training for the staff to help them be effective.

Finally, set target goals for access for students. More and more schools are getting students laptop computers that go back and forth between home and school. Many schools target a grade level for 100% saturation, so that all students have equal and ubiquitous access at school and home. Schools are beginning to leverage leasing programs from technology providers that include hardware, software, repair services, and even insurance in case of theft or damage. Most leasing programs provide a $1 buy-out clause, so the equipment can be transferred to the student for ownership at the end of a 3–5 year period, such as graduation. Check our Web site (www.technologystandards.com) for links to updated strategies for improving technology access, funding ideas, and providers.

Technology is new to my teaching. Where do I get started?

The best way to start integrating technology into education is to become a user for both professional and personal needs. Most educators get "hooked" by technology through the efficiency and joy of using email. Email usage alone accounts for a tremendous amount of "buy in" and comfort that educators have with technology as a tool for saving time and effort in staying connected with others.

From simple word processing and email, educators begin to mimic their students by playfully exploring other tools like spreadsheets, desktop publishing (newsletters), and/or electronic gradebooks. The exploration typically stems from personal or professional need to solve problems, save time, or simply from curiosity about all this "stuff" called technology. Combining the personal curiosity with formal training at in-services, university classes, or using "how-to" books allows educators to integrate technology into their teaching tool kit.

Probably the most important element to integrating technology is the willingness to take risks with your own learning. Set goals for yourself for using technology to automate tasks so you have more time with students, improve communication with parents, and/or expand learning opportunities for students with a variety of learning styles. Make sure that you're not doing technology for it's own sake. Ultimately, it's all about learning and teaching, so the best place to get started is through using technology on your own.

Why do we even have technology standards? We don't have pencil standards?

Technology standards offer schools an opportunity to focus attention on new skills and tools education. As we have emphasized in the book, technology standards have more to do with cognition and learning skills than simply learning technology. Technology standards create an important framework to discuss and act upon learning skills, as well as deal with the rapidly changing nature of information and knowledge in our society and world. It may be more accurate to consider technology standards as "knowledge worker"standards for students and educators.

The ISTE National Education Technology Standards are written for students, teachers, and administrators. One way to think about these groups is as people who research, communicate, manipulate, and create information and knowledge. Technology standards are the road maps of knowledge workers in schools, guiding the steps of their active inquiry, information management, and learning to learn skills. Technology Standards are important because they emphasize thinking skills over the tools.

My students know more about using technology than me…. what should I do?

It is easy for educators to feel that they must be masters of their classroom to be successful at helping students learn. It is important that educators be skilled within the pedagogy, content, and assessment of their particular discipline. But then, along comes information technology that turns the premise of the teacher as an all-knowing "sage" on it's head. Because of the nature of society, information, and technology, students have quicker access to more data (good and bad) than ever before in human history.

Technology evolves much faster than most educators

can keep pace. Students, on the other hand, are usually very adept at learning and using these new tools. Part of the reason may be rooted in the definition of technology as "...anything that did not exist when you were born." Most students don't consider TV, computers, and VCRs "technology," but these amazing toys allow them to play around learning. To most adults these technologies are "tools" that must be inventoried, studied, cataloged, and mastered. It's a pretty intimidating task for people whose plate is already full with curriculum, report cards, staff meetings, and parent communication.

The secret to being successful as a teacher around technology is to view yourself not (as a technology guru once put it) as the "sage on the stage," but the "guide on the side." The teacher's role can be as coach, facilitator, and "guide" as students navigate through their learning projects using the technology. Let the students be the "experts" on technology tapping into their natural curiosity, skills, and ease of learning how to use these information "toys." Students can teach each other and the teacher about using new software or technology. The teacher can then concentrate on the content and assessments. The result of these "learning partnerships" are powerful classroom environments in which the technology becomes a catalyst for new relationships to knowledge, communication, and each other.

What can we do to get our administrators more supportive of technology?

Most school leaders are motivated to improve the safety, efficiency, or the effectiveness of learning for students in schools. Principals and superintendents know that technology has a role to play in schools, but they may need help in understanding how it helps students learn and/or makes teachers more efficient at their jobs. They certainly want to be sure that safety and budgets are not being compromised by technology.

A good strategy for persuading not only administrators, but parents, school board, and community/business members as well, is to form a technology advisory group. This group can work together to develop a technology plan, budget, and strategy in support of making sure all students can achieve technology and other learning standards. Bringing key stakeholders together to form decisions and policy around technology will create important conversations and buy-in for adoption of technology standards.

As administrators get involved in these conversations, two things should begin to happen for them: 1) they will see stakeholders coming together to focus on important topics such as the effectiveness and efficiency of learning through technology, and 2) they will help lead the necessary changes in schools to accomplish the goals of the technology advisory group. These experiences will engage administrators in a process of change around improving schools for learning. Engaging an administrator in fulfilling their own dreams and goals for school, while involving other key stakeholders in the process, is probably the best way to get the support of technology for improving the learning environment.

How can my school use technology to form partnerships with other schools, businesses, or community groups?

Schools need to form relationships with other schools, businesses, and community groups to expand learning opportunities for students. These relationships are key to the school learning environments being relevant, connected, and continually improving. Technology can play a big role in building the bridges between schools and other groups. It's important that schools consider and use the technology to reach out, communicate, and build those relationships with others.

It would take an entire book to describe all the possible ways schools can use technology to form partnerships. One thing a school can do is seek out other schools or businesses with whom the school wants to form a partnership with an offer to help that partner. When a school seeks to form a relationship with a business the question, "What can our school do to help you?" is often met with disbelief. Businesses are usually asked what they can do to help schools. When the business learns that students are willing to help provide artwork, newsletter advertising, or do a Web page for the business using the school technology, they get very interested. The partners can negotiate mutual support with the ultimate goal of expanding learning opportunities for students.

Many other types of strategies using technology to form partnerships are possible. Consider establishing partnerships between schools in the same town via email to work on community service projects. Schools from other countries can link up through key pals, Web pages, and/or video conferencing to learn together. Schools can get together with other schools and businesses from many places to form coalitions for learning or service. Technology provides schools with gateways to form new relationships with other people and organizations. It's important that schools see that they can offer expanded learning opportunities for their students by carefully forming partnerships with others through the creative use of technology.

For a richer description and many examples of these kind of relationships, please check out the book *School/Business Partnerships — A Leader's Manual* (Visions, 2000) by Jim Utter and Mark Standley.

Conclusion

"I like the dreams of the future better than the history of the past."
      ~   Thomas Jefferson

There's an old story about a king who asked his wise men and women to boil down all the world's wisdom into one book. After 10 years of sweat and toil, they presented His Majesty with the single volume. Glancing through it, the king asked if they could now synthesize the book into a single sentence. After another 10 years, the group proudly presented the king with a wooden plaque containing the words "This too shall pass." After admiring the plaque for a few minutes, the king then asked the group to further reduce it down to a single word. After another 10 years these aged scholars dragged in a heavy stone for the king on which they had carved the word, "MAYBE."

It's an understatement—one that will come as no surprise to anyone reading this book—to say that technology is a rapidly moving target. Most three-year technology plans are obsolete after the first year of implementation. We simply don't know what is going to happen. Think about the implications that wireless technology, portable (and wearable) computers, open standards, and peer-to-peer sharing have for our schools. By the time our standards reflect these emerging technologies, what new ones will have appeared on the horizon?

Here is a very personal case in point. My oldest son— 16 at the date of this writing—remembers when the Internet was something new you could do with your computer. He doesn't remember a world without computers, but he does remember when the first graphical Web browser (Mosaic) opened up a whole new world of information and entertainment. Like most members of his generation, he was quick to absorb and lateralize this new medium, but he has clear recollections of not having it to do his schoolwork or communicate with his friends. However, my younger son, born five and a half years later, does not remember a world without the Web. Like television for most of the people in my generation, the Web has simply always existed for him. When he was six, a friend gave him a floppy disk with the shareware game Dirt Bike on it. He began to play the game, paused his bike in mid-jump, dialed up our ISP, launched Netscape and went to AltaVista, did a search for some game hints, logged off, and resumed his paused game armed with the new information he had found on the Internet. It never occurred to him that the information he sought would not be available, right when he wanted it, and on his own terms.

In the five and a half years between the births of my sons, the world changed dramatically. Since that time, the pace of change has been even more frenetic as we experience the early stages of the exponential growth of the Information Revolution. It's not over yet, by a long shot.

Can schools keep pace with this kind of change? Can technology standards evolve to reflect the rapid changes in technology?

The answer is really a point on which the survival of public schools hinges. If schools are able to adapt—to embrace standards not simply as items to be tested, but as new ways to think about and implement instruction—public schools will thrive. If standards can reflect not only the use of technology tools, but the new ways of communicating and of getting work done, then public schools will be preparing the population for the challenges of new economic and social structures.

This won't be easy. Many schools take what we consider to be a reactionary approach to standards—that is, they shoehorn their current practices and instructional methods into the standards framework, looking for areas in which they already meet the standards and therefore do not need to make substantive changes. We'd prefer to see schools accept standards as a challenge to examine instructional methodology, curriculum content, technology distribution, and staff development in an effort to establish long-lasting reform. When a government or military institution is attacked by terrorists or when a corporation's computers are hacked, those organizations examine every detail of their security measures, discard measures that are ineffective, improve on others, and add new measures as necessary based on current conditions. This is a good model for schools to follow in regard to standards. Public schools are being assailed on several fronts. Rather than retrenching, schools should examine their practices and forge new ones when necessary.

The other day I was showing a colleague a digital photo I had taken of a moose. The fall colors were spectacular, and the reflection off of the pond in which the moose was standing showed a glint of the low-hanging fall sun amid the colors of the birch and aspen trees. The moose' reflection was broken, but recognizable among the gentle ripples of the water's surface. My friend admired the bucolic scene.

Then, I showed him the original photograph. In it, the moose was standing by the side of the road, not in a pond. The fall colors were muted (it was a dark day) and somewhat indistinct. All in all, it was a fairly average photograph. The water in the photograph that I showed my friend, including the reflection, was added digitally in Photoshop using a simple filter. The colors were saturated and enhanced in a similar fashion, and the whole scene was sharpened to bring the colors into more focus. The idyllic scene, while having some basis in reality was, in fact, largely an illusion.

Technology is like that. It presents us with tremendous possibilities, but it calls into question what is real and what is not. Is the moose really standing in a pond? Is the person sending you email really a 12-year old student? Is the information about prescription medications that you found on Joe's House o' Healthcare Web site accurate? Do those hate groups that publish on the Web really mean what they say? Are we, perhaps, inventing new realities that we don't yet understand?

Knowing how to "work" technology tools is not enough. Our students need to understand and evaluate situations in which they find themselves. They need to know how to communicate, how to think for themselves, how to answer questions, and then ask more. They need to know what is real and what is not. They need to be connected to learning opportunities and resources inside and outside the school environment. This will take a lot of work and a lot of attitudinal changes, on their part and on our part as their teachers and mentors.

Technology standards should reflect the use of technology for understanding, communicating, and creating. In this sense, they are no different than other academic standards. We've made a good start. It's up to technology leaders in our schools and communities to maintain the momentum. There will always be changes along the way, so we should remember the king and wise scholars who were looking for final answers. We need to keep in mind the changing nature of technology and the new opportunities to improve learning opportunities for students of all ages.

Resources

www.technologystandards.com
Authors Web Site (for updates and more technology
standards resources)

Organizations

International Society for Technology in Education
480 Charnelton Street
Eugene, OR 97401-2626
Phone: 541.302.3778 or 800.336.5191
Email: iste@iste.org
Web: www.iste.org

ISTE Standards Publications used in this book & Ordering information (www.iste.org/bookstore)

1) *National Educational Technology Standards for Students — Connecting Curriculum and
   Technology*, 2000. ISBN 1-56484-150-1

2) *National Educational Technology Standards for Teachers*, 2000.
ISBN 1-56484-162-6

ISTE Collaborative Project

1) Technology Standards for School Administrators (TSSA)
   (www.iste.org)

The Collaborative for Technology Standards for School
Administrators (TSSA Collaborative) is leading an initiative to
develop and document a national consensus about what
PK–12 administrators should know about and be able to do to
optimize benefits of technology use in schools. This
consensus will be published by the Collaborative in October
2001 as Technology Standards for School Administrators

(TSSA). For more informration, contact TSSA Collaborative Chair, Jim Bosco at bosco@wmich.edu or Co-director of the Project, Heidi Rogers at hrogers@uidaho.edu.

International Technology Education Association (ITEA)
Technology for All Americans Project
1914 Association Drive, Suite 201
Reston, VA 20191-1539
Phone: 703.860.2100
Email: itea@iris.org
Web: www.iteawww.org

ITEA Publication used in this book

Standards for Technological Literacy: Content for the Study of Technology, 2000.
ISBN 1-887101-02-0

Consortium for School Networking
1555 Connecticut Ave, NW, Suite 200
Washington, DC 20036-1126
Phone: 202.466.6296
Email: info@cosn.org
Web: www.cosn.org

Other important titles used to prepare this book

Gooden, Andrea R. 1996. *Computers in the Classroom: How Teachers and Students are Using Technology to Transform Learning.* San Francisco: Jossey-Bass and Apple Press. ISBN 0-7879-0262-4

David Gordon, ed. 2000. *The Digital Classroom: How Technology is Changing the Way We Teach and Learn.* Cambridge, MA: The Harvard Education Letter. ISBN 1-883433-07-X

Haymore Sandholtz, Judith, Cathy Ringstaff, and David Dwyer. 1997. *Teaching with Technology: Creating Student-Centered Classrooms.* New York: Teacher's College Press. ISBN 0-8077-3586-8

Barbara Means, ed. 1994. *Technology and Education Reform: The Reality Behind the Promise*. San Francisco: Jossey-Bass Publishers. ISBN 1-55542-625-5

Ohler, Jason. 1999. *Taming the Beast: Choice and Control in the Electronic Jungle*. Bloomington, ID: Technos Press. ISBN 0-7842-0873-5

About the Authors

Warren W. (Skip) Via, Jr.
PO Box 25128, Ester, Alaska 99725
Voice: 907.479.4934

North Star Borough School District

email: svia@gci.net

Warren W. (Skip) Via, Jr., has been a teacher for 24 years, all but two of those years in Fairbanks, Alaska. For the past seven years he has served as an Instructional Technology Specialist for the Fairbanks North Star Borough School District. He co-chaired the Alaska Goals 2000 Technology Standards Committee, the group that developed Alaska's technology standards, and served on several statewide technology task forces. He was Alaska's invited teacher delegate to both Secretary's Conferences on Educational Technology in Washington, D.C. He serves on Apple Computer's National Education Advisory Council and was invited to work with the Milken Foundation to develop standards for teacher performance. He is a former Associate Editor of *The Catalyst* and has had articles published in several journals and magazines. His web design efforts have been recognized by Curriculum Administrator, from whom he received a Gold Award in 1999. Skip has traveled extensively throughout Alaska and other states conducting in-services and delivering keynotes to various school districts and conferences. He was honored with the Past Service award from the Alaska Society for Technology in Education for his contributions to the advancement of educational technology in Alaska.

Mark Standley
19913 Kalka Circle, Eagle River, Alaska 99577
Voice: 907.696.5335

Standby eResources

email: mark@standbyeresources.com

Mark Standley has been a professional educator, an author, and business executive in the computer industry in Alaska for more than 20 years. He works with Pacific Rim school leaders and communities providing training, projects, and resources to promote the effective use of technology in learning.

He co-chaired the Alaska Goals 2000 Technology Standards Committee. Mr. Standley is the author of several books on education and technology, including *The Technology Advisory Council* (ISTE, 1991), *School/Business Partnerships, Global Project-Based Learning with Technology, and Technology Standards* (Visions, 2000/2001), and *Future Courses: A*

About the Authors

Compendium of Thought About the Future of Technology and Education (TECHNOS, 2001). He has conducted leadership retreats for more than 20 years in Alaska, the Pacific Northwest, and Japan on subjects including cyber-schools, global project-based learning, digital storytelling, and school/business partnerships. He served as a teacher in the U.S. Peace Corps in South Korea.

Mr. Standley holds a M.S. degree in Education Technology from the University of Oregon. He lives with his wife, an artist, and their two children just outside of Anchorage, Alaska.